LUKE

BOOKS OF FAITH SERIES
Leader Session Guide

David L. Tiede

AUGSBURG FORTRESS
Minneapolis

LUKE
Leader Session Guide

Books of Faith Series
Book of Faith Adult Bible Studies

 Book of Faith is an initiative of the
Evangelical Lutheran Church in America
God's work. Our hands.

For more information about the Book of Faith initiative, go to www.bookoffaith.org.

References to ELW are from *Evangelical Lutheran Worship* (Augsburg Fortress, 2006).

Web site addresses are provided in this resource for your use. These listings do not represent an endorsement of the sites by Augsburg Fortress, nor do we vouch for their content for the life of this resource.

ISBN: 978-1-4514-0142-4

Writer: David L. Tiede
Cover and interior design: Spunk Design Machine, spkdm.com
Typesetting: Diana M. Running, Minneapolis, MN

The paper used in this publication meets the minimum requirements of American National Standard for Information Sciences—Permanence of Paper for Printed Library Materials, ANSI Z329.48-1984.

Manufactured in the U.S.A.
14 13 12 11 1 2 3 4 5 6 7 8 9 10

CONTENTS

Introduction

Book of Faith Adult Bible Studies

Welcome to the conversation! The Bible study resources you are using are created to support the bold vision of the Book of Faith initiative that calls "the whole church to become more fluent in the first language of faith, the language of Scripture, in order that we might live into our calling as a people renewed, enlivened, empowered, and sent by the Word."

Simply put, this initiative and these resources invite you to "Open Scripture. Join the Conversation."

We enter into this conversation based on the promise that exploring the Bible deeply with others opens us to God working in and through us. God's Word is life changing, church changing, and world changing. Lutheran approaches to Scripture provide a fruitful foundation for connecting Bible, life, and faith.

A Session Overview

Each session is divided into the following four key sections. The amount of time spent in each section may vary based on choices you make. The core Learner Session Guide is designed for 50 minutes. A session can be expanded to as much as 90 minutes by using the Bonus Activities that appear in the Leader Session Guide.

• Gather (10–15 minutes)

Time to check in, make introductions, review homework assignments, share an opening prayer, and use the Focus Activity to introduce learners to the Session Focus.

• Open Scripture (10–15 minutes)

The session Scripture text is read using a variety of methods and activities. Learners are asked to respond to a few general questions. As leader, you may want to capture initial thoughts or questions on paper for later review.

• Join the Conversation (25–55 minutes)

Learners explore the session Scripture text through core questions and activities that cover each of the four perspectives (see diagram on p. 6). The core Learner Session Guide material may be expanded through use of the Bonus Activities provided in the Leader Session Guide. Each session ends with a brief Wrap-up and prayer.

• Extending the Conversation (5 minutes)

Lists homework assignments, including next week's session Scripture text. The leader may choose one or more items to assign for all. Each session also includes additional Enrichment options and may include For Further Reading suggestions.

A Method to Guide the Conversation

Book of Faith Adult Bible Studies has three primary goals:

- To increase biblical fluency;
- To encourage and facilitate informed small group conversation based on God's Word; and
- To renew and empower us to carry out God's mission for the sake of the world.

To accomplish these goals, each session will explore one or more primary Bible texts from four different angles and contexts—historical, literary, Lutheran, and devotional. These particular ways of exploring a text are not new, but used in combination they provide a full understanding of and experience with the text.

Complementing this approach is a commitment to engaging participants in active, learner-oriented Bible conversations. The resources call for prepared leaders to facilitate learner discovery, discussion, and activity. Active learning and frequent engagement with Scripture will lead to greater biblical fluency and encourage active faith.

1 We begin by reading the Bible text and reflecting on its meaning. We ask questions and identify items that are unclear. We bring our unique background and experience to the Bible, and the Bible meets us where we are.

5 We return to where we started, but now we have explored and experienced the Bible text from four different dimensions. We are ready to move into the "for" dimension. We have opened Scripture and joined in conversation for a purpose. We consider the meaning of the text for faithful living. We wonder what God is calling us (individually and as communities of faith) to do. We consider how God's Word is calling us to do God's work in the world.

2* We seek to understand the world of the Bible and locate the setting of the text. We explore who may have written the text and why. We seek to understand the particular social and cultural contexts that influenced the content and the message. We wonder who the original audience may have been. We think about how these things "translate" to our world today.

Devotional Context

Historical Context

Lutheran Context

Literary Context

4 We consider the Lutheran principles that help ground our interpretation of the Bible text. We ask questions that bring those principles and unique Lutheran theological insights into conversation with the text. We discover how our Lutheran insights can ground and focus our understanding and shape our faithful response to the text.

3* We pay close attention to how the text is written. We notice what kind of literature it is and how this type of literature may function or may be used. We look at the characters, the story line, and the themes. We compare and contrast these with our own understanding and experience of life. In this interchange, we discover meaning.

* Sessions may begin with either Historical Context or Literary Context.

The diagram on p. 6 summarizes the general way this method is intended to work. A more detailed introduction to the method used in Book of Faith Adult Bible Studies is available in *Opening the Book of Faith* (Augsburg Fortress, 2008).

The Learner Session Guide

The Learner Session Guide content is built on the four sections (see p. 5). The content included in the main "Join the Conversation" section is considered to be the core material needed to explore the session Scripture text. Each session includes a Focus Image that is used as part of an activity or question somewhere within the core session. Other visuals (maps, charts, photographs, and illustrations) may be included to help enhance the learner's experience with the text and its key concepts.

The Leader Session Guide

For easy reference, the Leader Session Guide contains all the content included in the Learner Session Guide and more. The elements that are unique to the Leader Session Guide are the following:

- **Before You Begin**—Helpful tips to use as you prepare to lead the session.
- **Session Overview**—Contains detailed description of key themes and content covered in each of the four contexts (Historical, Literary, Lutheran, Devotional). Core questions and activities in the Learner Session Guide are intended to emerge directly from this Session Overview.
- **Key Definitions**—Key terms or concepts that appear in the Session Overview may be illustrated or defined.
- **Facilitator's Prayer**—To help the leader center on the session theme and leadership task.
- **Bonus Activities**—Optional activities included in each of the four sections of "Join the Conversation" used by the leader to expand the core session.
- **Tips**—A variety of helpful hints, instructions, or background content to aid leadership facilitation.
- **Looking Ahead**—Reminders to the leader about preparation for the upcoming session.

Leader and Learner

In Book of Faith Adult Bible Studies, the leader's primary task is facilitating small group conversation and activity. These conversations are built around structured learning tasks. What is a structured learning task? It is an open question or activity that engages learners with new content and the resources they need to respond. Underlying this structured dialog approach are three primary assumptions about adult learners:

- Adult learners bring with them varied experiences and the capability to do active learning tasks;
- Adult learners learn best when they are invited to be actively involved in learning; and
- Adults are more accountable and engaged when active learning tasks are used.

Simply put, the goal is fluency in the first language of faith, the language of Scripture. How does one become fluent in a new language, proficient in building houses, or skilled at hitting a baseball? By practicing and doing in a hands-on way. Book of Faith Adult Bible Studies provides the kind of hands-on Bible exploration that will produce Bible-fluent learners equipped to do God's work in the world.

Books of Faith Series

Book of Faith Adult Bible Studies includes several series and courses. This Luke unit is part of the Books of Faith Series, which is designed to explore key themes and texts in the books of the Bible. Each book of the Bible reveals a unique story or message of faith. Many core themes and story lines and characters are shared by several books, but each book in its own right is a book of faith. Exploring these books of faith in depth opens us to the variety and richness of God's written word for us.

Luke Unit Overview

The Gospel of Luke invites readers—including us—to explore the story of Jesus and his mission as God's Chosen One (Messiah). From the joyous accounts of Jesus' birth in a manger in Bethlehem to the stark images of his crucifixion at Golgotha to the "eye-opening" meal at Emmaus, we are invited into a remarkable story. The evangelist (the writer of Luke) describes how God has broken into our world and history by sending the one who is Messiah and Savior. In these eight sessions, you and your class will explore eight key texts in the life of Christ and search for the meaning and truth revealed in them.

Session 1 (Luke 2:1–20) asks, "Why Was Jesus Born?" In the most familiar of the Christmas birth narratives, Luke's story reveals that Jesus' birth is really about God's reign coming to earth. The "timeless truth" of the story is more compelling because it is "timely." Jesus was born in a real time and place, in an occupied country where all threats to imperial authority were fiercely suppressed.

Session 2 (Luke 2:21–40) asks, "What Will Become of This Child?" The infant Jesus signified that God's promises would be fulfilled, even in the face of opposition. Simeon and Anna witness that the child signifies the fulfillment of God's promises for Israel's consolation and Jerusalem's redemption. But the infant Jesus will also be a sign of the rejection of God's purposes by God's own people. Thus, only God knows what will become of God's people because of the Christ child.

Session 3 (Luke 4:14–30) declares, "Let God Be God!" God of the Bible is not under our control. This story reveals the reign, or mission, that God is bringing into the world through the Messiah, Jesus. As we hear this story in Christian congregations, the direct question confronts us, "If Jesus is the Messiah, are we ready to receive his reign as he defined it?"

Session 4 (Luke 7:1–17) asks, "What Was Jesus Doing?" As God's Messiah and prophet, Jesus went about Galilee, preaching, teaching, and healing, and he commissioned his disciples to continue those actions in his name. This session focuses on Jesus' raising the son of a widow and healing a centurion's servant. The gospel does not promise that Jesus' followers will be immune from sickness and death, but Jesus provides glimpses of the life and healing that God intends for all who trust in him.

Session 5 (Luke 9:18–36) asks, "Why Must Jesus Die?" Jesus was understood to be the fulfillment of God's promises to Israel, responding in scriptural terms to the question "Who is Jesus?" But as we get all of those titles straight, the enduring question becomes "Why did Jesus have to die?" Jesus was no victim of fate or politics. Jesus was driving the action forward. He was enacting God's script.

Session 6 (Luke 15:1–32) declares, "And Grace Will Lead Me Home." Taken together, the stories of the lost sheep, the lost coin, and the lost son draw us into the world of God's love for the lost. But we are also alerted to the controversial nature of Jesus' ministry that stretched the bounds of Israel's law and angered its religious leaders. How will we respond when we confront the lost or those who may not "fit" our picture of God's proper people?

Session 7 (Luke 23:26–49) asks, "Ah, Holy Jesus, How Hast Thou Offended?" This session focuses on the events leading up to Jesus' crucifixion. The execution of Jesus tested all of God's promises of justice and mercy. Standing at the foot of the cross, we are both tormented and deeply inspired by what we see and hear.

Session 8 (Luke 24:13–35) asks, "How Did Jesus' Resurrection Change the World?" Jesus' resurrection is not simply a fact from the past. It is a transformative event. "I want to know Christ," says Paul, "and the power of his resurrection" (Philippians 3:10). Luke's story leads us deeply into how the experience of Jesus' resurrected presence turned fearful followers into apostolic witnesses.

Luke 2:1–20

Leader Session Guide

Q Focus Statement

When Jesus was born, God entered our earthly lives.

Key Verse

To you is born this day in the city of David, a Savior, who is the Messiah, the Lord.
Luke 2:11

Focus Image

He Qi, "Nativity"
© He Qi. Used by permission.

Why Was Jesus Born?

Session Preparation

Before You Begin . . .

An old saint once noted, "Christians can be so heavenly minded they are no earthly good!" But Luke's story of Jesus' birth is about God's reign coming to earth. Imagine holding an infant in your arms. Think about the human, earthy, physical details of caring for a baby, and consider the promise that God has for the world in every child. Now, suppose you are Mary, holding Jesus. What do you believe God has in mind for the earth?

Session Instructions

1. Read this Session Guide completely and highlight or underline any portions you wish to emphasize with the group. Note any Bonus Activities you wish to do.

2. If you plan to do any special activities, check to see what materials you'll need, if any.

3. Have extra Bibles on hand in case a member of the group forgets to bring one.

4. Set up a nativity scene. Do not include the magi, because they are not in Luke's telling of the nativity story.

Session Overview

The "Christmas Gospel" is an excellent place to begin the eight sessions on Luke. Most people are familiar with the story and often connect personal memories with it. What are your earliest memories of hearing the story? Who told it to you? Who were you with? People have happy and sad Christmas memories. In the hymn "O Little Town of Bethlehem," we sing, "The hopes and fears of all the years are met in thee tonight!" You already know how the story goes, but as you move together in the coming sessions, listen with Mary and ponder in your heart how God's purposes will unfold in Jesus' life. And how about the unfolding story of your life? Where will Jesus' story meet the hopes and fears of your life and the lives of all the participants?

LITERARY CONTEXT

Luke's story is praised for its "timeless beauty," and it has been loved through the centuries and all over the world. Imagine staging a Christmas pageant in a place where people had never heard the story, perhaps among a remote tribe in the Amazon forests. How would you tell the story (plot, characters, messages) to reveal its richest truth about what God was doing through Jesus' birth?

We don't know as much as we'd like to know about how people learned Israel's scriptures, but the stories in Luke 1–2 about the miraculous births and childhoods of John and Jesus in are almost a running commentary on the stories of Samuel and David in the book of 1 Samuel. Mary's praise of God (Luke 1:46–56) even echoes the prophetic speech made by Samuel's mother Hannah in 1 Samuel 2. For those who remembered Samuel and David, the stories of John and Jesus revealed God's completion of the story that God began long ago. Both stories are filled with clues that God had a particular kind of king in mind. Bethlehem is a powerful connection between the stories. As you read aloud from those two stories (1 Samuel 16:1–13; Luke 2:4, 2:15), listen for Bethlehem as the place where God is at work.

HISTORICAL CONTEXT

All of the Gospels are continually mentioning the Roman occupation of the land. More than the other three, however, Luke's Gospel repeatedly sets the story of the nativity against the backdrop of the empire, explicitly mentioning three **emperors**— Augustus Octavian (Luke 2:1), Tiberius Caesar (3:1), and Claudius (Acts 11:28; 18:02; 23:26)—as well as numerous local governors, procurators, high priests, and kings appointed by Rome. The "timeless truth" of the story is more compelling because it is "timely." Jesus was born in a real time and place, in an occupied country where all threats to imperial authority were fiercely suppressed.

Luke's story does not advocate subversive activity or overthrow of the Roman order, and Jesus' birth does not appear to have attracted attention from the empire. (Compare that with Herod's response in Matthew 2.) At the same time, it must be noted that loyalty tests in the Roman order included required public affirmations that Caesar is Lord; Octavian was given the honorary title of "Augustus" (his name in our story) and was widely acclaimed as the Savior. One public monument dated just before Jesus' birth acclaimed Octavian as "filled with a hero's soul," making wars to cease so that "the Epiphany of Caesar" surpassed all his predecessors and any who would follow. "The birth date of

? Emperors:

After fierce wars between Mark Antony and Octavian for control of the empire, the Roman Senate proclaimed Octavian as emperor, or Caesar, and then gave him the honorary title of Augustus (the honored one). Israel's rulers were traditionally called kings and were anointed for office. The Romans insisted that only they could decide who was named king in Judea. Luke makes us aware of the importance of titles for both Octavian/Augustus and Jesus/Christ.

our god," declares the inscription, "has signaled the beginning of the good news for the world."

Into this historical context, the angels proclaim, "To you is born this day in the city of David a Savior, who is the Messiah, the Lord" (Luke 2:11). At this point in the story with Zechariah and Elizabeth gone, the shepherds, Mary and Joseph—and we who are reading—are the only mortals who know that Jesus is truly God's king, **Lord, Savior**, and Messiah. As you read, imagine what the Romans and their collaborators will think if the angels' words get out. How will Pilate and Herod respond when Jesus heads toward Jerusalem? And after Jerusalem is destroyed, how will the Roman authorities regard Jesus' followers? Those outcomes are foreshadowed in this opening announcement of Jesus' birth.

Lutheran Context

This session provides an excellent opportunity to focus on reading the Bible for what shows forth Christ. Lutherans talk about how all Scriptures points to Christ. This approach welcomes the popular call to "keep Christ in Christmas," which is no small task when the holiday has become so thoroughly commercialized. The participants will learn a wonderful truth when their homes are more filled with the Spirit of Christ in the Christmas season. Taking time to explore that could start a rich discussion because people already sense how important the Christmas season is.

As you discuss this story, keep the word *Christ* connected with the words *Messiah* and *King* because Jesus was born to be the Christ/Messiah/Anointed King. At the same time, don't worry about getting it all figured out too quickly. These are political titles, but Jesus will give them new meaning. In his meditation on Mary's **Magnificat**, Luther advised the prince to let the youthful Mary counsel him in governing well. Luther did not claim to be an expert in governance, but he understood that Mary was speaking as a prophet, telling the world how God reigns through King Jesus.

The world's political forces are often tempted to believe that they are ultimate or divine, rather than seeing that they are actually using mortal methods. Caesar is not truly the Savior or Lord. The Lutheran tradition has also been dubious about high-sounding "Christian" politics, whether of the "Holy Roman Empire" or some modern claim to be God's own party. Politics need to support and provide good governance—which is a worthy human

 Lord, Savior:

Both of these titles had been used for centuries by the rulers of the empires to assert the divine legitimacy of their reigns. In protest of the divine claims over Israel of the Babylonian Nebuchadnezzar, the prophet Isaiah quoted God, saying, "Before me no god was formed, nor shall there be any after me. I, I am the Lord, and besides me there is no savior." (Isaiah 43:10–11). When the angels declared Jesus to be the Savior, Lord, and Messiah, they were again declaring God's dominion over the empires.

Magnificat:

This Latin word identifies Mary's poetic song in Luke 1:46–55 that began, "My soul magnifies the Lord." Mary's song is powerful, echoing the prophetic song of Hannah over the birth of Samuel. Both women were speaking of God's might, especially in raising up the lowly and bringing down the high and mighty.

vocation in making the world a more trustworthy place—but be wary of those who claim divine rights or presume that God is on their side.

The Lutheran tradition is equally suspicious of secular claims that God has no place in human politics or economics. The prophets continued to call all leaders and governments to God's high standards of justice and mercy, and Luke's story revealed Jesus to be God's vessel of ruling the world. If the word *Christ* becomes too spiritualized, we miss the power of God coming in the flesh. At the same time, if the word *king* becomes too politicized, we forget that God is at work in the midst of—and often in the face of—Caesar's empire, yet never captive to its claims.

In our story, Bethlehem is more than symbolically significant. It existed for a thousand years before Jesus, and it continues to be a real town two thousand years later. If you visit the "Christmas square" today in Bethlehem, you will find the Evangelical Christmas Lutheran Church alive in faith and active with education and health care for Palestinian families, but under great duress. This congregation is a sign of Jesus' reign as they speak of "continuing Christ's ministry of preaching, teaching, and healing in his home country." Bethlehem, the birthplace of Jesus and David, is still a historic crossroads. Look up the Web site http://www.elcjhl.org/cong/bethlehem.

DEVOTIONAL CONTEXT

How can we feel the power of such a familiar story? Its beauty may make it seem sentimental, but it is a prophetic message of the Lord in our lives and for our world. The news is that when Jesus was born, God entered our earthly lives. Is that news promising or threatening? It is certainly life-changing, and world-changing!

Maybe the power of the story will hit you immediately, but don't pretend something for yourself or others. None of us really controls our feelings, and we are certainly not empowered to control the feelings of other people. The Book of Faith approach is an exercise in trusting the Spirit to touch our lives and those of all the participants in God's ways and time. Give the group time to wonder together about how they hear this old, old story in new ways.

The journey through Luke's story is just beginning, and it begins with gentleness and strength. Right at the start, we can sense with Mary and the shepherds that God is on the move. The details of our daily lives are illumined in the new light of Christ's presence with us! Not everything we have been doing looks good. In fact, we may be worried about secrets or deceits we hope God might not see, even when we know better. At the same time, God has entered our earthly lives. If we follow Jesus, where will he take us? Or send us? Back to our flocks? At least for now, but what then? Luke's larger narrative will continually testify that God has not come just to expose us but to empower us. We are being swept into God's great mission of love for the world. When God has entered our lives, each of us and all of us together are called and sent.

Facilitator's Prayer

Lord Jesus, you were born among us to bring God's reign into our world. Come into my life, reign in my mind, my heart, my will that I may know the blessing of your presence. And make me an agent of your mercy and your righteousness in all that I am and do. Empower all in our study of Luke's Gospel with your Spirit that they will grasp anew the wonder of your birth, bringing your kingdom into the midst of the kingdoms of the world. In your holy name. Amen.

Gather (10–15 minutes)

Check-in

Take time to greet each person, and invite learners to introduce themselves to one another. This first session on Luke is also a significant moment to extend special hospitality to newcomers, to welcome all as Christ among us.

Pray

Pray or sing these verses from a hymn by Martin Luther.

Welcome to earth, O noble Guest,
through whom this sinful world is blest!
You turned not from our needs away;
how can our thanks such love repay?

For velvets soft and silken stuff
you have but hay and straw so rough

Tip:
Nametags are almost always a good idea; even people who know each other can forget names, and newcomers may be called by name more easily. Christmas nametags could be useful, but the story is not about Christmas trees or wise men, so try to find images of shepherds, angels, or the manger scene that are in line with Luke's script.

Tip:
Invite participants to join you in praying three verses from Martin Luther's Christmas hymn, "From Heaven Above." These lines need to be savored. You could pray them together, but be cautious of asking people to take turns reading aloud because some readers might struggle. Consider asking a capable reader or accepting a volunteer to lead the group. The poetic phrases are a powerful witness to be heard. If you have a clear solo voice in the group, you might ask that person to sing these verses as your prayer.

on which as king so rich and great
to be enthroned in humble state.

Ah, dearest Jesus, holy child,
prepare a bed, soft, undefiled,
a quiet chamber in my heart,
that you and I may never part.
Amen.
("From Heaven Above." *Evangelical Lutheran Worship* 268, verses 8, 11, 12)

Focus Activity

Suppose a non-Christian friend asked you, "Why in the world was Jesus born in a stable?" Using only two minutes, write down the first things you would say.

Open Scripture (10–15 minutes)

In order to hear the story with fresh ears, consider bringing this text to life in one of the following ways:

1. Ask three to five people to be a "family" in which the children gather on Christmas Eve and the father or the mother reads the story to them. Encourage all the others to listen as if it were their family. What do they hope the children will hear? What power does the story itself have when parents read it to their children in their homes?

2. Set up your own "nativity pageant" with a narrator, Mary, Joseph, a baby, an "angel of the Lord," and a "heavenly host" to recite the appropriate lines. At first, this will seem like the usual Christmas pageant, but for this activity, ask the other participants to listen as if some of them were Jewish residents of Bethlehem and some of them were Roman officials.

3. Imagine staging a Christmas pageant in a place where people had never heard the story, perhaps among a remote tribe in the Amazon forests. How would you tell the story (plot, characters, messages) to reveal its richest truth about what God was doing through Jesus' birth?

Read Luke 2:1–20.

- What words or phrases caught your attention in this familiar story?

Tip:

Provide paper and pens or pencils for participants. Assure them that no one will be required to share what he or she writes, but encourage them to help get the conversation going. After participants have finished writing, take a few minutes to explore any thoughts or ideas they have. Welcome whatever they say! Write down notes on chart paper or a whiteboard.

Tip:

With advance preparation, you may find a way to darken the room before the reading and then illumine the scene suddenly at the moment when "the glory of the Lord" shone around the shepherds. In this birth, God entered our earthly lives.

Tip:

This session includes several suggestions for activities, and you may find some helpful. Make sure, however, that you take your time, treasure some moments for quiet, and give people the chance to dwell deeply in the wonder of this story. Calm and reflective moments are precious opportunities for people to experience God's presence.

- How do you sense God's reign "in the highest heaven" coming to earth?
- How do you imagine the shepherds felt when they returned to their flocks?

Join the Conversation (25–55 minutes)

Literary Context

1. The Gospel according to Luke is famous for its literary beauty, and this story is widely loved, even among people who know very little about Jesus or the Christian faith. Although the author's identity is never revealed, the first four verses of the book (Luke 1:1–4) acknowledge that many others have written accounts and emphasize that our author is intent on telling "the truth concerning the things about which you have been instructed."

- Luke 2:1–20 supplies the script that is re-enacted in Christmas pageants in every nation on earth, but this passage isn't only for children. Look again at the lines delivered by the characters in the story. For you, which voices announce the truth of what God is doing here? How do you imagine those voices sounding?

2. Luke's story of Jesus' birth follows wonderful accounts of angelic announcements to Zechariah (Luke 1:13–19) and Mary about God's purposes in the births of John and Jesus (1:28–37). The story also echoes with old scriptural accounts of the birth of Samuel (1 Samuel 1:1—2:10), who anointed David as Israel's king. The Hebrew word for the "anointed one" is *Messiah*, and the Greek word is *Christ*.

- Why is Bethlehem called "the city of David"? See 1 Samuel 16:1–13.
- God took David "from the sheepfolds" where he was tending sheep (Psalm 78:70–72) to anoint him as the shepherd king of Israel. Notice that the angelic messengers explicitly mention "the city of David" as the birthplace of "a savior, who is the Messiah, the Lord" (Luke 2:11). What clues do you get in the story about the kind of king that Jesus will be?

3. Mary plays a powerful role in Luke's story. The angel Gabriel tells her that she will bear this holy child. As God's faithful servant Mary declared, "Let it be with me according to your word" (Luke 1:38). She also prophesied that Jesus would fulfill the promises that God had made to Israel (Luke 1:54–55). Mary was silent in this story, but she "treasured all these words and

 Bonus Activity:

Compare Mary's *Magnificat* in Luke 1:46–55 with Hannah's prophetic speech in 1 Samuel 2:1–10. Invite learners to work in pairs or groups of three so they can have both readings open at the same time. Alternatively, you could present the two passages side by side by projecting them or making a handout. Ask participants to note similarities and jot them down on chart paper.

Bonus Activity:

Invite participants to discuss the role that Jesus seems to play in modern culture. How has culture's attitude changed regarding Jesus and the celebration or recognition of his birth? This topic can be a touchy one for many. Some may feel that culture has lost much of the sense of having or celebrating Christ in Christmas. Others may say that changes are good and reflect the more diverse nature of our culture. This activity is not intended to cause debate or argument, but it is likely a topic that is close to the surface in many communities.

Palestine in Jesus' Time
Lutheran Study Bible, p. 2109

Tip:

The distance is about 70 miles (113 km) in a straight line, but the walking route would have been somewhat longer, likely south along the Jordan Valley and Jericho before turning east toward Bethlehem.

Tip:

The purpose of this historical section is to remember that Jesus was not born in a fictional "once upon a time," but in a real time and place.

pondered them in her heart" (Luke 2:19). She would soon hear "a sword will pierce your own soul too" (see Luke 2:35).

• Luke's account of Jesus' birth causes believers and unbelievers to join Mary in wondering, "What in the world will become of this child?" How does Mary's response of treasuring and pondering these words prepare you for all that lies ahead in Luke's story of Jesus?

4. With which character or characters do you most closely identify in the story of Jesus' birth? Why?

Historical Context

1. Note the following places on the map of Palestine in Jesus' time: Nazareth, Galilee, Bethlehem, Judea, and Syria. How far did Joseph and Mary have to travel on their trip from Nazareth to Bethlehem? Imagine taking the journey by foot or on a donkey when about nine months pregnant.

2. Luke regularly alerts the reader to what is happening in the Roman Empire and in the local governance of Roman and Jewish authorities (see Luke 3:1–2; Acts 18:2). Here he mentions the "registration" of the whole empire by Caesar Augustus (probably for taxation and military conscription) and identifies Quirinius.

• Why do you think information about the Roman emperor and governor are explicitly given in the story?

3. The official Roman messengers proclaimed the "good news" that Caesar was the "savior," and all citizens were required to declare, "Caesar is lord!"

• What do you imagine the Romans might have thought if they heard that God's messengers (the angels) had announced that the "good news" was the birth of Jesus, "a Savior, who is the Messiah, the Lord" (Luke 2:11)?

• Why are those public titles for Jesus still "good news" for our time?

4. Historians believe that by the late first century (when Luke's Gospel was written), the Roman armies had already destroyed Jerusalem, burned the temple, and killed or taken Israel's leaders into slavery.

- In the midst of troubled times when Luke's story was first read, how do you expect the story of Jesus' birth renewed people's hope in God?

- How does the Christmas gospel continue to be especially powerful in times of sorrow or suffering in your family, or in the world? How do suffering people still find hope in this wonderful story?

Lutheran Context

1. Martin Luther compared the Bible to the straw-filled manger that held the Christ child. Lutherans speak of the Bible as the book that reveals Jesus Christ to us. What message about Jesus is "revealed" in this text from Luke? Who has revealed Christ to you most clearly in your life?

2. God's living word speaks both God's law and God's promise, sometimes bringing judgment and again announcing hope. God's word exposes how we have turned away from God, and yet it also reveals God's love and care for us.

- Take a few minutes to think about the past week. What if the angels interrupted your life just as they surprised the shepherds? What would you want to hide from God? What hope would their message give you?

3. Martin Luther was a biblical scholar who understood that the power of the four Gospels lies in their faithfulness to the one gospel that is the good news of what God has done for us in Jesus Christ. Luther wrote:

> Such a story can be told in various ways; one spins it out, the other is brief. Thus, the gospel is and should be nothing else than a chronicle, a story, a narrative about Christ, telling who he is and what he did, said, and suffered—a subject which one describes briefly, another more fully, one this way, another that way. ("Brief Introduction on What to Look for and Expect in the Gospels," Martin Luther's Basic Theological Writings, ed. Timothy Lull, Minneapolis: Fortress, 1989, p. 105).

- Read Matthew's story (Matthew 2:1–18) of Jesus' birth. Notice how the cruety of Herod the Great threatens to overshadow the joy of what God is doing. Both Luke and Matthew are telling the

 Bonus Activity:

That God chose to come to earth—to be with humanity in the form of a baby born in a manger—is both remarkable and unexpected. Invite learners to imagine other ways that God might have decided to break into our lives or to bring life and salvation. Ask learners to tell or even draw a picture of how this might have happened. Then reflect on what difference it makes that God came in this humble way.

 Tip:

When Luther spoke of the "theology of the cross," he emphasized how the story of Jesus is "down to earth," not only in its earthy details about shepherds and taxation but also in the profound sense of God dwelling with human beings in the midst of our difficulties.

Bonus Activity:

Imagine staging a Christmas pageant in a place where people had never heard the story, perhaps among a remote tribe in the Amazon forests. How would you tell the story (plot, characters, messages) to reveal its richest truth about what God was doing in through Jesus' birth?

Tip:

Be sure to pause and listen if participants tell about what they are suffering or if they express that their hearts have been touched while hearing about someone else's struggles. That could be the most "teachable moment" in your group's understanding of why God has come among us.

gospel truth of Jesus. Describe how each evangelist opens your heart and mind to understand Jesus' birth.

Devotional Context

1. Take another look at the Focus Image on p. 5. How is it similar to or different from other images of Christ's birth? What is most striking to you about this image?

2. We opened our session with verses from Luther's Christmas hymn, "From Heaven Above." It echoes one of the deepest convictions of the Reformation that God has acted to justify and save us. The Gospel story is about how God came to earth among us, and not about our spiritual ascent to God. The Gospel according to John (1:14) declares, "The Word became flesh and lived among us."

- Take a few minutes to reflect on your family's Christmas traditions. Many are good family fun, but some may bring everyone closer to God's intention. Write down one or two ways that observing Christmas could highlight the good news that Jesus' birth means "God is with us."

3. Both Luke and Matthew highlight that Jesus, God in the flesh, was born into a displaced, refugee, or undocumented family.

- Take time to pray for all the work that is done among refugees in the name of Christ by our congregations, Lutheran Social Ministries, Lutheran World Federation, and Lutheran Immigrant and Refugee Services.

- How can you see yourself embodying the good news of Jesus in the world?

4. People have happy and sad Christmas memories. In the hymn "O Little Town of Bethlehem" we sing, "The hopes and fears of all the years are met in thee tonight!" You already know how the story goes, but as you move together in the coming sessions, listen with Mary and ponder in your heart how God's purposes will unfold in Jesus' life. And how about the unfolding story of your life? Where will Jesus' story meet the hopes and fears of your life?

Wrap-up

1. If there are any questions to explore further, write them on chart paper or a whiteboard. Ask for volunteers to do further research to share with the group at the next session.

2. Strongly encourage the participants to begin the daily readings, as outlined in the enrichment sections of their learner guides.

Pray

Lord Jesus, you came as God among us and as an infant in a poor family dislocated by the kingdoms of the world. God's promises for a ruler and Savior all came true in you. You are our Savior and Lord, God who has come among us. Help us be as joyful as the shepherds and join the angels in giving thanks to God. Empower us by your Spirit to tell the world of your love, and give us courage and hope to serve within your reign in this world and the next. We pray in your blessed name, Lord Jesus. Amen.

Extending the Conversation (5 minutes)

Homework

1. Read the next session's Bible text: Luke 2:21–40.

2. Take out a manger scene from Christmas storage and put it on your TV, monitor, newspaper, or wherever you get the news of the world. Leave the "wise men" in the box for now, and simply pray the Lord's Prayer for God's kingdom to come on earth as in heaven. With your family or others, discuss how God's kingdom came to earth, and consider what will happen next in Luke's story when the world's rulers find out.

3. Re-read Luke 2:1–20 with special attention to verse 19: "Mary treasured all these words and pondered them in her heart." Which words do you treasure most in the story, and how do you ponder them in your heart and live them?

Enrichment

1. If you wish to read through the entire book of Luke during this unit, read the following sections this week.

  Day 1: Luke 1:1–25

  Day 2: Luke 1:26–38

  Day 3: Luke 1:39–56

  Day 4: Luke 1:57–66

  Day 5: Luke 1:67–80

  Day 6: Luke 2:1–20

  Day 7: Luke 2:21–40

Tip:
Encourage learners to reflect during the coming week on how their lives are blessed because God came among us when Jesus was born.

Tip:
Encourage the participants to keep a journal of their thoughts and prayers as they do the daily readings. You may wish to provide a low-cost notebook or journal that people could bring along to future sessions.

2. Do an Internet search for "images of nativity" or "images of the birth of Jesus." Make note of any images that are especially appealing or interesting to you. You might also consider looking at Christmas scenes from around the world at the following Web site: http://campus.udayton.edu/mary/gallery/creches/crechesworld.html

For Further Reading

The Gospel According to Luke by Michael Patella in New Collegeville Bible Commentary Series (Collegeville, MN: Liturgical Press, 2005). Presents a very accessible commentary to help people read the whole story.

"Session 1: Caesar and Lord" in *Learning Luke: The Apostolic Gospel* by David L. Tiede and friends (selectlearning.org, 2009). A twelve-session video series with study guides on how Luke's story empowers God's mission.

Provoking the Gospel of Luke: A Storyteller's Commentary by Richard W. Swanson (Cleveland: Pilgrim Press, 2006). Provides dramatic clues for presenting the lectionary readings from Luke.

Augsburg Commentary on the New Testament: Luke by David L. Tiede (Minneapolis: Augsburg Fortress, 1988).

Looking Ahead

1. Read the next session's Bible text: Luke 2:21–40.

2. Read through the Leader Guide for the next session and mark portions you wish to highlight for the group.

3. Make a checklist of any materials you'll need to do the Bonus Activities.

4. Pray for members of your group during the week.

Luke 2:21–40

Leader Session Guide

Focus Statement

Every newborn reveals God's love and prompts wonder about the future. The infant Jesus signified that God's promises would be fulfilled, even in the face of opposition.

Key Verse

My eyes have seen your salvation, which you have prepared in the presence of all peoples. Luke 2:30–31

Focus Image

© Design Pics / SuperStock

What Will Become of This Child?

Session Preparation

Before You Begin . . .

This story is like the overture to a symphony in which the key themes are sounded, then each movement that follows deepens what was heard at the beginning. Simeon and Anna are real human characters in the story, but they appear as prophets and then are never heard from again. It is not as important to try to "get inside their heads"—which modern authors often do—as it is to absorb God's word as it is spoken through them.

Session Instructions

1. Read this Session Guide completely and highlight or underline any portions you wish to emphasize with the group. Note any Bonus Activities you wish to do.

2. If you plan to do any special activities, check to see what materials you'll need, if any.

3. Have extra Bibles on hand in case a member of the group forgets to bring one.

Session Overview

"God only knows what will become of this child!" That is often said in desperation when a young person has frightened parents or elders, but it can also be a declaration of awe when a child is remarkably gifted. In Luke's story, God does know what will become of the child Jesus, and Simeon and Anna witness that the child signifies the fulfillment of God's promises for Israel's consolation and Jerusalem's redemption. But the infant Jesus will also be a sign of the rejection of God's purposes by God's own people. Thus, only God knows what will become of God's people because of the Christ child.

LITERARY CONTEXT

This session gives the participants an opportunity to appreciate how Luke's Gospel draws us back into the scriptural story of God's love for Israel and then points us forward to Jesus' enactment of God's reign. God's promises are about to be fulfilled in this child, but such a mission won't be easy, even for God. Both the conflict and the cost will be immense.

Like the story of Jesus' birth, Luke's account of the presentation of Jesus in the temple invites dramatization. The staging of the setting and characters are all about royal birth. Imagine a television special about the christening of a new heir to England's throne; in comparison to that, the drama about Jesus is less grandiose but his reign is profoundly more important. In one case, a long line of limos brings the royal family to the welcome of thousands; in this story a peasant girl and her rustic husband are stunned when elderly prophets welcome their child royally at the temple.

Make sure Simeon and Anna's prophetic words ring through any pomp and ceremony. The whole world is watching as they announce Jesus as the fulfillment of the people's hopes for God's promised **consolation of Israel** and **redemption of Jerusalem**. Simeon also declares the depth of the conflict that is to come. The dramatization will leave all of us wondering: "What is God doing?" "What will become of this child?" "What will become of us?"

The Learner Session highlights the prophetic answers to those questions, but prophetic testimonies are poetic, open to what actually happens next. Pay attention to the content of Simeon's first pronouncement along with Anna's prophetic words. Notice how deeply hopeful those words sound when you place them in the context of the script. God means it all for good. Then don't miss Simeon's second prophetic message. The plot of the full story of Luke's Gospel is built upon God's action encountering human rejection.

HISTORICAL CONTEXT

This rich story invites readers to think first about the historical moment within the story when Simeon and Anna welcomed the infant Jesus in the temple. They prophetically declared that God was enacting the promises for which Israel had longed hoped. Yet how did their prophetic words sound in the late first century when Luke's narrative was written and read? By then, people knew what had actually happened to Jesus and the dire fate of the temple was also part of history. The Romans had destroyed it while putting down the Jewish rebellion in 70 CE Luke testifies that God's promises will not fail. How is that true?

Take some time to let the participants explore what they hear in Simeon and Anna's rich prophetic words. You may find helpful to do the bonus activity about maps (p. 26 of this guide) and

---

? The Consolation of Israel:

This phrase recalls such rich prophetic promises as Isaiah 40:1–5, made famous in Handel's Messiah: "Comfort, O comfort my people, says your God. Speak tenderly to Jerusalem."

? The Redemption of Jerusalem:

This phrase echoes Mary (Luke 1:46–55) and Zechariah's (1:68–79) earlier prophecies concerning God's visitation and redemption of God's people. See also Joseph of Arimathea, "waiting expectantly for the kingdom of God" in Luke 23:50–51; Cleopas and an unnamed disciple hoping that Jesus "was the one to redeem Israel" in Luke 24:21 and Acts 1:6.

to explore the key terms with the broader prophetic meanings of these words. But don't get lost in the historical details, as fascinating as they are. Help the participants feel the profound confidence that Simeon and Anna had in God's promises in the midst of real suffering. Their faith will become all the more powerful when Luke's whole story of Jesus is told.

Remember that virtually all of Jesus' first followers were Jews, whether from Judea or Galilee. The apostle Paul, who was known as the apostle to the Gentiles (the non-Jewish nations), was thrilled by the numbers of non-Jews who came to believe in Jesus, yet he was also emphatic that non-Jews who believe that Jesus is Messiah are in no position to boast before God against Jews who don't believe that Jesus is the Messiah (Romans 11:13-20). Even Simeon's harsh second prophecy announced that the "falling of many in Israel" would precede the "rising of many in Israel." Again Luke's story as a whole will shed light on how Jesus ultimately means promise, not threat, to Israel and to the world.

Lutheran Context

"Faith," declares the letter to the Hebrews (11:1), "is the assurance of things hoped for, the conviction of things not seen." Among Lutherans, the Bible is called the "Book of Faith" because it conveys the assurance and conviction of God's faithfulness, even when God's trustworthiness can't be proven or perhaps even seen. **Prophecy**, therefore, refers to speaking confidently of God's faithfulness to what God has promised, even speaking God's own messages when God's Spirit has empowered the speaker to do so. Biblical prophecy is not mere **prediction**, because God continues to be at work in what happens next.

Therefore, the mystery of the Bible as the word of God is deep because God is alive, and God's word is alive to the changes in the world and the changes in people's lives when they come to faith in God. God's word is also fearsome in its consequences for those who turn away from God. When Luther, following Paul and Isaiah, emphasized that faith comes by hearing, he was also emphasizing—as Paul did—that the Holy Spirit gives the ability to trust God, even when we can't pin God down by our own reason or strength. "The letter (meaning "the written code") kills," says Paul, "but the Spirit gives life" (2 Corinthians 3:6).

 Prophecy/prediction:

Prophecy literally means "to speak forth." *Prediction* means to announce in advance. Biblical prophecies often included predictions, especially in the warnings that people who chose not to turn to God would perish. The great biblical prophets were authorized to speak for God: "Thus says the Lord!"

DEVOTIONAL CONTEXT

Lutherans speak with confidence of the "real presence" of Christ in the Lord's Supper. Trusting that Jesus Christ is true to his word, we are awed when we receive the bread and wine with the words, "This is the body of Christ, broken for you. This is the blood of Christ, shed for you." Sometimes, those wonderful words become routine among us, but when your group "[discusses] with each other why faithful people can be so moved by what they have seen, heard, and tasted in the Lord's Supper," invite participants to tell stories from their own lives or from the experiences of others.

This session is about seeing and believing, prompting us to wonder which comes first. We are not told how Simeon recognized Jesus as the Messiah when he saw this infant being brought into the temple among many others. Trusting in the Holy Spirit, he clearly believed, then saw. And he saw God's promises about to be kept while Jesus was still a babe in arms. The gospel song "Open the Eyes of My Heart, Lord" expresses one of the reasons we close our eyes when we pray. Encourage the participants to be aware of what they "see and hear" when they listen to the story or pray with closed eyes.

Facilitator's Prayer

Come, Holy Spirit, open the eyes of my heart that in the infant Jesus, I may believe and see your love and care for me and for those whom I am called to lead. Your consolation will heal me, reaching deep into my sorrows and struggles. Your redemption is my hope, even when you expose my efforts to seek my own advantage. Teach me, Holy Spirit, to see in Jesus the promise of the Father and to follow every step of his ways as the gospel story unfolds. In God's holy name I pray. Amen.

Gather (10–15 minutes)

Check-in

Invite learners to share completed homework or any new thoughts or insights about the previous session. Be ready to give a brief recap of that session if necessary, and take a few minutes to describe how chapters 1 and 2 of Luke prepare us for the whole story of Jesus. The songs of Zechariah, Mary, and the angels tell us what God is about to do. In In today's session, Simeon and Anna will also announce how Jesus is about to bring in God's

Tip:
Encourage people to share their pictures of their children or grandchildren. If someone has a photo of an infant in the arms of an elderly person, perhaps that can be your Simeon or Anna picture for this session.

reign and they will alert us to the opposition to God's will that Jesus will expose.

Pray

Living God, we who are young and we who are old pray for your Holy Spirit to rest on us. Open our eyes and hearts to see your promises kept in the children you have given us, and may our hope be renewed in the future you brought to us through the infant Jesus. Amen.

Focus Activity

Look at the Focus Image. Imagine who is holding the infant, and imagine who the infant is. Then imagine that the older person is asking, "What will become of this child?" Have you ever held a child and asked that question? What hopes and fears lay behind it for you? Share your thoughts with at least one other person.

Open Scripture (10–15 minutes)

You might consider asking the participants to close their eyes during this reading. One of the mysteries of the story is how Simeon and Anna's faith gave them the eyes of the heart to recognize or "see" God's promises about to be fulfilled in this infant.

Read Luke 2:21–40.

- How do you imagine Simeon's voice sounded when he praised God for letting him live to see this child who fulfilled God's promises?
- What feelings or emotions do you think different characters may have been feeling in this story?
- What questions are raised for you as you listen to this text?

Join the Conversation (25–55 minutes)

Literary Context

1. This story stands at the center of the first two chapters of Luke's Gospel, introducing Luke's whole narrative. Both Simeon and Anna speak prophetically in this story, and Anna is explicitly called a prophet. Prophecy often includes an element of prediction, but the primary force of prophetic speech is the announcement of God's word and will. Look closely at 2:25–28.

Tip:
Ask a volunteer to pray this prayer.

Tip:
An alternative would be to ask a grandparent to bring an infant grandchild to the class, and invite him or her to begin the activity with the question, "What will become of this child?"

Tip:
All children are God's children, and we seldom know what might prove to be "special" about the life of any infant. In the times of monarchs, royal children regularly received great attention. In our story, Jesus is recognized as the ruler—the royal child—that God is about to install.

Tip:
A large Bible (perhaps a large pulpit Bible) would set a grand and solemn tone for this reading. Perhaps even a procession of the readers in robes would help people to sense the temple grandeur of the story.

Bonus Activity:
Consider reading the entire story aloud, using a narrator and characters to read the appropriate lines. Perhaps an elderly pair could be Simeon and Anna, welcoming a younger couple with an infant. Simeon's direct words in verses 29–32 and 34–35 could be recited by an elderly man, and Anna's script in verses 36–38 could be recited by an elderly woman. Discuss: How does seeing and hearing the text affect the way you understand the message and the situation?

Tip:

Point out that the Holy Spirit touches Simeon three times in Luke 2:25–28. That is a clue that God is at work, helping the blind Simeon to "see" with eyes of faith.

Tip:

Anna uses the word *redemption* to describe the "rising" of Jerusalem. God's redemption has to do with forgiveness and a fresh start.

Bonus Activity:

Edward Gibbon's *The History of the Decline and Fall of the Roman Empire* (1776) and William L. Shirer's *The Rise and Fall of the Third Reich* (1960) are classic histories written to explain how and why those empires fell. Ask participants to name other empires or individuals who rose and fell dramatically. What contributed to the rise and fall of each? Is there a common theme among these stories? How can God bring a "rising," or redemption, in the presence of evil?

Bonus Activity:

Many Bibles and atlases have good maps of the city of Jerusalem with details about the temple (examples: "Jerusalem in Jesus' time" in the map section of *HarperCollins Study Bible*; the diagrams of the temple in *Lutheran Study Bible*, pp. 1696–1697). Tourists in modern Israel are also shown models of first-century Jerusalem, including the temple, with detailed descriptions of how the Romans breached the walls, slaughtered the inhabitants, and eventually burned the temple. Simply displaying such maps, models, or depictions can be a good way to help people understand how profound Simeon and Anna's prophetic words would have sounded after the Romans destroyed the temple in 70 CE.

- What clue does Luke give about Simeon that helps us know that what he says about Jesus in 2:29–32 is true?
- How are his words similar to those of the angel in 2:10–11?

2. Notice how Simeon's first words (2:29–32) are all in praise or blessing of God for God's faithfulness to the salvation promised by the prophets. He is speaking of Jesus. To what people will Jesus be a "light"? To what people is he given for their "glory"? As you look forward to Luke's whole story, what do you think this will mean?

3. Simeon's second prophetic message, spoken as a blessing of Mary and Joseph, is surprisingly harsh. Now we know that God knows Jesus' mission is not going to be easy. Jesus will expose human defiance of God's will. As the plot of Luke's story moves forward with Jesus bringing God's reign on earth, what sort of resistance, refusal, and rejection will he encounter? Who will resist him? What will God do then?

4. Notice the sequence when Simeon announces 1) "the falling" and 2) "the rising of many in Israel." This is not a story of the rise and fall of an empire, but a prophetic diagnosis of how even after many of God's people have stumbled and fallen, God will bring about a rising. What word does the prophet Anna use to describe this "rising" (2:38)? What does that word mean for you?

Historical Context

1. This is one of Luke's many scenes in the Jerusalem temple. The temple was more than a large church building, even more than a national cathedral. It was understood as the dwelling place of God, where God's hovering presence assured the nation's safety. Even the Romans usually stayed away from its most holy precincts. By the time Luke's Gospel was written, the Roman conquest of Jerusalem in 70 CE was probably a painful memory, etched with accounts of the slaughter of the priests at the altar.

- Notice how Simeon was "looking forward to the consolation of Israel" and Anna joined those "who were looking for the redemption of Jerusalem." Christians rightly observe that Jesus was not merely "a political messiah," but were Simeon and Anna's hopes fulfilled? Do you think God's promises failed when the Romans destroyed Jerusalem? How is Jesus a sign of hope even when the forces of evil appear to triumph?

2. Notice how when Mary and Joseph "had finished everything required by the law of the Lord," they returned to Nazareth. Joseph, Mary, Simeon, and Anna were all faithful to God's law, and Jesus was born in Judea and raised in Galilee.

• Some Christian commentaries on Luke call it "The Gentile Gospel." Luke makes fewer references than Matthew to Hebrew or Aramaic words, and the scriptures that Luke read were probably written in Greek, but the story is still about Israel. The word *Gentile* means "nations." What do you think it means that the glory of God's chosen people is—and has always been—to be a light to the nations of the world?

Lutheran Context

1. Martin Luther was an Old Testament scholar. His commentaries on Genesis and the Psalms illustrate that he was deeply aware of the living God. His interpretations of the New Testament are filled with Israel's Scriptures. Thus, the Book of Faith is also about the whole Bible, and Simeon and Anna are almost Old Testament characters because their appearances took place when Jesus had not yet been anointed for his mission. They embody Israel's best faith: confident of God's promises, now welcoming the infant Messiah, and deeply aware that this child will face hard things.

• How do Simeon and Anna inspire you to trust God's promises, even though you may not see the complete fulfillment of those promises in your lifetime?

• Have you wondered why parents and grandparents often have tears in their eyes when they bring their infants for baptism? How are their hopes and fears like those of Anna or Simeon?

2. Lutheran Christians are aware that sin is turning away from God or even opposing God. Even as we seek to trust in God's mercy, we are still caught in our own schemes, self-interests, and sin, so we find ourselves resisting or defying God, even when we want to do better. We yearn for the purity of heart to welcome Christ Jesus into our lives, yet we also realize that we benefit from economic and political systems that may guard our privileges more than they protect the vulnerable who live among us.

• If Christ Jesus appeared in the here and now of your community, so that "the inner thoughts of many [would] be revealed" (Luke 2:35), what personal or public parts of your life or your community do you think people would not want him to see?

 Tip:

Notice how Jesus' name was given at his circumcision in accordance with what Gabriel told Mary in 1:31, but Simeon was not given any historical clues about who this child is.

 Tip:

Point out how the Holy Spirit is identified in verses 25, 26, and 27 as guiding Simeon to "see" the Lord's Messiah before he had "seen death." Then in verse 30, he declares that his "eyes have seen" God's salvation.

 Bonus Activity:

Luther refers to the concept of two kingdoms when talking about how God's reign "plays out" in the world. The kingdom on the left is about government and other institutions that God uses to keep order and ensure that justice is done. The kingdom on the right is about our spiritual existence. Through this kingdom, God brings the good news of Jesus Christ, transforming us into "saints" called to live out our call to love of neighbor. Discuss how God can be at work in either "kingdom."

Tip:

Post a copy in the room of Luther's explanation of the third article of the Apostles' Creed and perhaps recite it aloud.

Tip:

This story is filled with the deep faith of Israel and is alive with the promise that Israel's calling is to be a light to all the nations. This touches the sacramental life of a congregation, its ministry among the elderly, and its outreach.

Bonus Activity:

If you are meeting in a church, consider gathering around the altar, listening to an elderly person tell about a personal experience of the presence of God. What words of hope and prayers of protection would he or she have for his or her grandchildren or for babies being baptized?

Bonus Activity:

Ask the participants to close their eyes while someone reads Acts 2:17, which is a direct quotation from the prophet Joel. Heaven's windows opened for Simeon and Anna. What are the dreams, visions, and prophecies of God's sons and daughters in our time?

3. In his explanation of the third article of the Apostles' Creed in the Small Catechism, Martin Luther speaks of the Holy Spirit as the one who "has called me through the gospel, enlightened me with his gifts, made me holy, and kept me in the true faith . . ." As you look back at the role of the Holy Spirit in this text, how does this definition of the Holy Spirit seem to fit? In what way does the Spirit call to you through the message of this passage?

Devotional Context

1. Simeon's praise of God has been rehearsed throughout Christian history. The Latin phrase *Nunc dimittis* means "Now you are dismissing." We often sing Simeon's song as we depart from the Lord's Supper. In some Christian communities, such as certain places in China, people often weep as they leave the Lord's table.

- Discuss why it is that faithful people can be so moved by what they have seen, heard, and tasted in the Lord's Supper.
- Have you ever been deeply touched with a sense of God's presence?

2. Simeon's song is regularly sung in funerals for elderly Christians. Ancient Christian artists often depicted Simeon with tears flowing from his physically blind eyes. They believed that when he said, "My eyes have seen your salvation," he "saw" with the eyes of his trusting heart, just as elderly people often die trusting promises they will not "see."

- When have you experienced the profound witness of this song?
- How has the faith of someone who has died helped you to trust God in your life?

3. What do you suppose Mary was feeling when Simeon declared that Jesus would be a "sign that will be opposed" and that "a sword will piece [Mary's] own soul too"? If you are a parent, when have you experienced concern or fear over what may lie ahead for your child? What helps you to face those fears?

4. How can Christ's followers continue Israel's calling, or vocation, to be a light to the nations?

Wrap-up

1. If there are any questions to explore further, write them on chart paper or a whiteboard. Ask for volunteers to do further research to share with the group at the next session.

2. Ask the participants to write down the name of an older person, living or dead, who brought the light of God into their lives. Invite them to tell themselves the best way to be grateful for that person.

Pray

O Lord, now let your servant depart in heav'nly peace,
for I have seen the glory of your redeeming grace:
a light to lead the nations unto your holy hill,
the glory of your people, your chosen Israel.

Then grant that I may follow your gleam, O glorious Light,
till earthly shadows scatter, and faith is changed to sight;
till raptured saints shall gather upon that shining shore,
where Christ, the blessed daystar, shall light them evermore.
("O Lord, Now Let Your Servant Depart in Heav'nly Peace,"
ELW 313)

Extending the Conversation (5 minutes)

Homework

1. Read the next session's Bible text: Luke 4:14–30.

2. Many congregations observe the practice of giving a candle for families to light on the anniversary of a baptism. They usually refer to Jesus' words in Matthew 5:14–16: "You are the light of the world . . . let your light shine before others, so that they may see your good works and give glory to your Father in heaven." Write down the names of a) a person who was recently baptized; b) someone who was baptized many years ago; and c) yourself. Light a candle and pray for the light of Christ to shine in those lives and in the lives of all the baptized to the glory of God.

3. Reread Simeon's blessing of Jesus' mother and father and his dire warning to Mary (Luke 2:34–35). From what you already know about the story, imagine the times when Mary's soul was pierced by what happened to Jesus. How does Simeon's prophecy prepare us for what is coming?

Tip:
Bring the focus back to elderly people and infants as signs that God goes ahead of all of us into the future.

Tip:
Simeon's song, which is called the *Nunc dimittis*, is our closing prayer. You might ask an elderly person to speak it or invite the whole group to sing it.

Enrichment

1. If you wish to read through the entire book of Luke during this unit, read the following sections this week.

   Day 1: Luke 2:41–52

   Day 2: Luke 3:1–6

   Day 3: Luke 3:7–14

   Day 4: Luke 3:15–20

   Day 5: Luke 3:21–38

   Day 6: Luke 4:1–13

   Day 7: Luke 4:14–30

For Further Reading

The Gospel According to Luke by Michael Patella in New Collegeville Bible Commentary Series (Collegeville, MN: Liturgical Press, 2005), pp. 19–22.

"Session 2: Prophecy and History" in *Learning Luke: The Apostolic Gospel* by David L. Tiede and friends (selectlearning.org).

Provoking the Gospel of Luke: A Storyteller's Commentary by Richard W. Swanson (Cleveland: Pilgrim Press, 2006), pp. 97–100.

Augsburg Commentary on the New Testament: Luke by David L. Tiede (Minneapolis: Augsburg Fortress, 1988), pp. 72–79.

"Introduction to Luke" in *Lutheran Study Bible* by Richard W. Swanson (Minneapolis: Augsburg Fortress, 2009), pp. 1694–1695.

Looking Ahead

1. Read the next session's Bible text: Luke 4:14–30. It might be a good idea to do the daily readings as well (see Enrichment #1 above).

2. Read through the Leader Guide for the next session and mark portions you wish to highlight for the group.

3. Make a checklist of any materials you'll need to do the Bonus Activities.

4. Pray for members of your group during the week.

5. Prepare yourself for the shift we will take now from looking forward to the promise Jesus' life holds to observing how he inaugurates and embodies his reign as God's Messiah with his words and deeds.

Luke 4:14–30

**Leader
Session
Guide**

Focus Statement
Today is God's time!

Key Verse
Today this scripture has been
fulfilled in your hearing!
Luke 4:21

Focus Image

© *Ikon Images/SuperStock*

Let God Be God!

Session Preparation

Before You Begin . . .

This is the first session where Jesus steps up to his full role as
Messiah. Don't be quick to judge the people in Nazareth who first
spoke well of him, then became angry. Once you feel the force of
what Jesus is announcing, you may also find yourself looking for
reasons to discount or explain away what he is saying. Note that
everything Jesus is saying is what God said earlier through the
prophets. What if God means it for now?

Session Instructions

1. Read this Session Guide completely and highlight or underline
any portions you wish to emphasize with the group. Note any
Bonus Activities you wish to do.

2. If you plan to do any special activities, check to see what
materials you'll need, if any.

3. Have extra Bibles on hand in case a member of the group forgets
to bring one.

Session Overview

Mark Twain once commented that the parts of the Bible he
couldn't understand didn't bother him as much as the parts of the
Bible he could understand. His comment was probably cynical, but
it is also good counsel for Christians to pay attention to the stories
that may disturb them, because the God of the Bible is not under
our control. This story reveals the reign, or mission, that God is
bringing into the world through the Jesus the Messiah.

LITERARY CONTEXT

When reading a novel, it is often helpful to identify the character
or active agent who moves the story forward. This is the
"protagonist," while the "antagonist" is the character who resists
this action or rejects the protagonist. The first exercise that has
been proposed for the participants is intended to identify the Holy
Spirit or God as an active agent in Luke's story. Jesus' assertive
behavior in this story is not due to his personal psychology, but he
is operating with the authorization of God.

After the participants have underlined the words *Holy Spirit*, you might ask them, "Who is moving this story forward? How do you sense the connection between what Jesus is doing and his being 'full of the Holy Spirit,' 'led by the Spirit,' and 'filled with the power of the Spirit' (Luke 4:1,14)?"

The four-reader exercise in the participant materials is intended to highlight the central message from the prophet Isaiah. If you look up the passage in Isaiah, you will discover that some words appear to come from Isaiah 58:6, but most are directly taken from Isaiah 61:1–2. Perhaps those verses were once written together in the scroll that Jesus read or in Luke's copy of Isaiah. Now, as we read them in unison, Jesus announces them as the program of his reign. When the scroll is rolled up and Jesus is seated to teach, he makes it clear that his reign starts now.

Scholars have long struggled to understand what exactly happened in Nazareth. Luke's account of the encounter is much more detailed than the account by Mark or Matthew (see Mark 6:1–6; Matthew 13:54–58). The first report in Luke 4:22 that "all spoke well of him and were amazed at the gracious words that came from his mouth" may suggest that they were glad to hear him reading from Isaiah and were confident that the prophet's "gracious words" were God's promises to them. But in announcing, "Today this scripture has been fulfilled in your hearing," Jesus identified himself in the role of the "anointed one" or Messiah (4:18), and declared the inauguration of the long-awaited **Jubilee.** When they questioned Jesus' claim by saying, "Is not this Joseph's son?" they were also rejecting the fulfillment that Jesus was bringing. Then Jesus appealed to prophetic precedents. God's promises would still be kept, just as they had been with Elijah and Elisha, but not for those who thought they were entitled because they were God's chosen people. Instead Jesus declared that the prophetic blessings went to the outsiders first.

Luke's literary skill is also evident in Luke 7:22–23, where Jesus recites what he did after he left Nazareth. He was clearly fulfilling the Messiah's mission as stated in Isaiah 61.

The identifying of Jesus' harsh words in 4:23–27 is intended to help participants feel the force of Jesus' prophetic judgment on "insiders" who assume the promises are for them. If you use this exercise, don't try to soften the blow. That is the point of the question, "How would you feel if Jesus spoke like this in your congregation?"

> **?** *Jubilee:*
> In Leviticus 25:8–12, Israel was directed to celebrate a jubilee every fiftieth year as a season of liberation of people from their bondages, the restoration of the families and properties, and a holy return to God. When this proved difficult to do without disrupting the whole economy, the hope grew that God would eventually declare the jubilee, perhaps when the Messiah had come.

HISTORICAL CONTEXT

Most study Bibles include maps of Palestine (including Galilee and Judea) as well as the Roman Empire, often tracking the journeys of Paul as reported in the Acts of the Apostles. It may be helpful to point out that the temple, which was the location of activity in the previous session, stood only in Jerusalem, but **synagogues** were spread like local congregations throughout Palestine and the whole Roman world because Jewish communities were scattered in what was called the **diaspora.**

Modern Jewish synagogues are descendants of these early centuries, just as twenty–first century Christian congregations trace their histories through many eras. In the book of Acts, several of the sermons of the apostles were delivered in synagogues in order to testify to Jews and Greeks that Jesus was the Messiah. A few modern Christian congregations include Jewish people who believe that Jesus is the Messiah of God's reign, but the division primarily about whether Jesus is truly the Messiah continues between the assemblies called synagogues and the assemblies called churches. The ways the scriptures are read in these assemblies is remarkably similar in ancient and modern assemblies.

The material in this section is historically interesting, but don't get lost in playing Bible times. As we hear this story in Christian congregations, the direct question confronts us: "If Jesus is the Messiah, are we ready to receive his reign as he defined it?"

LUTHERAN CONTEXT

The Learner Session Guide focuses on the deep Lutheran convictions that God's word is a "two edged sword" of command and promise, law and gospel. This usage of the word "law" highlights the experience that we have when even words of promise can provoke our distrust or expose our self–interest that are threatened by God's authority. This use of the word *gospel* was also emphatic for Martin Luther when he was blessed to hear God's mercy for him while he was still a sinner, set against God. God's "gospel" called him to trust this promise, to let go of control, to let God be God.

Jesus' sermon in Nazareth, therefore, is "truth telling" of the kingdom of God, whether or not we feel ready to hear it. The first move is to admit that Jesus' program makes us uneasy or even angry when we discover that we will not be given privileges we

? *Synagogues:*

This term is derived from the Greek word for a "gathering" or "assembly," and it is used in all kinds of languages to identify the local Jewish house of study or house of prayer. Archeological remains of Jewish synagogues have been found throughout modern Greece, Italy, Turkey, Iran, Iraq, Egypt, and Palestine.

? *Diaspora:*

This term, derived from the Greek word for "scattering," describes how Jewish communities were spread throughout the Babylonian, Egyptian, Greek, and Roman Empires. The destructions of the temple by the Babylonians (597 BCE) and the Romans (AD 70) accelerated that scattering, but Jewish communities often thrived in the midst of the empires. The Christian mission moved first among those communities.

might think we deserve, "after all the good things we do for God." The second move is to receive the promise embodied in Jesus: pure grace from the Messiah, granting release, forgiveness, and recovery of sight through following Jesus and his Messianic mission.

The activities suggested in the Learner Session Guide are intended to let people feel both the threat to our self-righteous lives and the promise of the word of God, healing and liberating us, personally and as a community. Most recovery programs, such as Alcoholics Anonymous, are built on this lesson of "let go and let God!" Perhaps someone in your group could tell about how AA communicates this deep assurance. Make sure you get to the miracle of freedom that occurs when we live into Jesus' program without needing to justify ourselves.

On the personal side, you might ask further, "When was there a time in your life when you thought you had the whole world in your control? What would you have thought about Jesus' words at that time?" Or again, "When did you most feel your need for God, even when you didn't deserve love or justice? How did Jesus sound to you then?"

On the community experience, you might recall a story from the history of your congregation or from a source such as The Lutheran magazine that might tell of a group that was caught up in the freedom of the gospel to spread the good news or to be of help to their neighbors. Help people explore the feeling of this freedom, enacting God's reign of mercy and justice toward those who need it without pride or judging whether they were worthy.

Devotional Context

At first, this story will not feel very "devotional," because its prophetic force is awesome. It might be a good exercise to recall your catechism when you routinely said, "We should fear and love God so that . . ." and then invite participants to let the power of this story touch them with God's holiness. When the word of Christ dwells in you richly (Colossians 3:16), the living Christ is with you, in you, among you. And Jesus is Lord, so devotion yields with awe into the obedience of love. This story reveals God's love, now at work through the Holy Spirit in Jesus, bringing release to the captives, recovery of sight to the blind, liberation to the oppressed, and the restoration of God's Jubilee.

To fear and love such a God is an act of faith and Christian freedom, only possible through trusting that Jesus will do what he says. Living into this faith as a community is also a practice of Christian freedom. This means that Bible study is not only applying the letter of the law to our lives, but also welcoming the presence of the living God into our reading, hearing, and dwelling in God's word. Using this story to justify ourselves by judging the people of Nazareth is contrary to the promise that Jesus embodies and will now enact in the story. He simply "passed through the midst of them" when they were intent on killing him because his mission was to enact God's saving mercy, even for those who intended evil. As Peter announced in Acts 2:36: "God has made him both Lord and Messiah, this Jesus whom you crucified."

Facilitator's Prayer

Lord Jesus, I pray for the presence of your Spirit with the group and me as we enter the fearsome and wonderful story of your reign as Messiah, beginning in your hometown of Nazareth. Your gracious words from the prophet Isaiah ring with promise for us and for the world, but we are also warned against claiming privileges. Open our hearts to receive the strength and grandeur of your reign without needing to control your mission. Empower us to be agents of the mercy and justice you bring to those who need it most. In your holy name I pray. Amen.

Gather (10–15 minutes)

Check-in

You could spark the imagination of the participants by staging the "check-in" as a welcome for distinguished guests and diplomats to an inauguration. People could choose their identities at the door or you could assign their roles. As they are ushered to their seats, someone could announce, "The Prime Minister of Washburn Middle School," "The Queen of Quilting," etc.

Invite learners to share completed homework or any new thoughts or insights about the previous session. Be ready to give a brief recap of that session if necessary.

 Tip:
Some participants may object that this session is "too political." Don't worry about it if their problem is with Jesus, because this story reveals that the kingdom that Jesus brought was intended to make a profound difference on earth. Be careful, however, not to get caught in a partisan political discussion. Jesus cannot be co-opted by any political party. The deeper question will continue well beyond this session: WWJD— What would Jesus do?

Pray

Lord Jesus, you have come among us in the majesty of God's mercy and justice. We are hopeful for your reign among us and eager to hear your word for us. To tell the truth, we are also worried about all you may have in mind. We often prefer that you would just bless what we have going, confirming our special place in God's family. But we know you have larger plans for the world, greater love for our neighbors, and costly calls to us. We pray, therefore, for your Holy Spirit to open our hearts, our minds, and our lives to hear, obey, and enact your will in all that we say and do. In your name, we pray. Amen.

Focus Activity

At the top of a sheet of paper, write "Jesus is Lord!" Then draw a vertical line down the center of the page. Put a plus sign at the top of the left column and a minus sign on the right. Why are you glad and what makes you uneasy that Jesus is Lord? In what way is this confession a "plus" (left)? In what way might it be a "minus" (right)? Write one or two thoughts on each side of the line. Share your thoughts with one or two others in your group.

Tip:

Search for "the Isaiah Scroll" or "the Great Isaiah Scroll" on the Internet for information about the most complete scroll from the time of Jesus, discovered in 1947 at Qumran near the Dead Sea. Made of seventeen strips of leather sewn together, that massive scroll might be like the scroll from which Jesus was reading in Nazareth.

Bonus Activity:

Consider asking someone to make a "scroll" from which the passage will be read. The scroll could be made simply by printing the passage on pieces of paper taped together, but make it long enough that you can "unroll the scroll" in front of the group.

As an alternative, consider listening as the whole story is read by a volunteer against the backdrop of a picture of the installation of a new president or prime minister. In this scenario, the people are a national assembly of workers, children, diplomats, and armed forces.

Open Scripture (10–15 minutes)

This would be a good session for a dramatic reading of the passage. Ask everyone to stand as if they were the congregation in Nazareth. Identify one person to play the role of Jesus and one to play the role of the synagogue attendant. The narrator could stand to one side or even use a microphone from off stage. You will need a "scroll" from which "Jesus" can read the Isaiah text and a chair where he will sit down to speak. The "members of the congregation" will need to play out their roles of first welcoming Jesus and his words, then getting cautious, then becoming angry to the point of trying to haul him away. After the Jesus character has passed through their midst, use these questions for a few minutes to explore the experience.

Read Luke 4:14–30.

- What did you hear in Jesus' words that inspired you?
- What did Jesus say or do that made you uncomfortable?
- Why do you suppose the people became so angry?

Join the Conversation (25–55 minutes)

Literary Context

1. Luke is sometimes called "The Holy Spirit Gospel," and the book of Acts is often called "The Acts of the Holy Spirit." The writer, sometimes called the evangelist, set the stage for the beginning of Jesus' ministry in Nazareth by frequent references to the Holy Spirit. We saw that three times in the story of Simeon in our previous session (Luke 2:25–35). Take a pencil and underline the words "Holy Spirit" or "Spirit" in the following texts:

- Luke 3:21–22; Acts 10:38 (Jesus is baptized.)
- Luke 4:1–13 (Jesus is tempted by the devil.)
- Luke 4:14–16 (Jesus' ministry begins in Galilee.)

In your own words, describe what you see God doing in the story.

2. Take time to appreciate how carefully the scene is set for Jesus' very brief message. Read the following condensed version of the story to focus on all of Jesus' actions, zeroing in on Isaiah's prophecy, centering on Jesus' word:

READER #1: Then Jesus, filled with the power of the Spirit, returned to Galilee.

READER #2: He began to teach in their synagogues. He went to the synagogue on the Sabbath day.

READER #3: He stood up to read.

READER #4: He unrolled the scroll and found the place where it was written:

ALL: The Spirit of the Lord is upon me, because he has anointed me to bring good news to the poor. He has sent me to proclaim release to the captives and recovery of sight to the blind, to let the oppressed go free, to proclaim the year of the Lord's favor.

READER #4: He rolled up the scroll and gave it back to the attendant.

READER #3: And sat down.

READER #2: The eyes of all in the synagogue were fixed on him.

READER #1: Then he began to say to them:

ALL: Today this scripture has been fulfilled in your hearing.

Bonus Activity:

A "concordance" is a great tool for Bible study. This resource book makes note of nearly every occurrence of specific words in a particular translation of the Bible. A concordance–type search for specific words in various versions of the Bible can now be done very rapidly using most kinds of Bible study software. That tool does not work well in paraphrase Bibles because those versions don't try to represent each word from the Hebrew or Greek manuscripts. Encourage someone to do a concordance search of the words "Spirit" and "Holy Spirit" in the Gospel of Luke and in the Acts of the Apostles. Show the list of all the passages to the group, then encourage them to look up 10 passages in Luke's Gospel and 10 in the book of Acts to discover how thoroughly the Holy Spirit is the motivating force in the story.

Tip:

Do not "assign" readers, because someone may feel uncomfortable or inadequate as a reader. Ask for volunteers to read the parts.

Tip:

Invite learners to look back at the map of Palestine in Session 1, p. 8 in the Learner Session Guide. Ask them to take note again where Nazareth is located in relation to Jerusalem.

Tip:

If you have access to a projector and can display images, you might consider downloading and displaying pictures or drawings of ancient synagogues. Make an Internet search for "ancient synagogues." For an example, visit this site: www.jewishmag.com/44mag/synagogues/synagogues.htm

Bonus Activity:

Encourage someone to make a display about ancient scrolls, perhaps gathering books on the Dead Sea Scrolls from Qumran, handwritten Bibles, and so on. The Saint John's Bible is a modern handwritten and illuminated edition of the NRSV, and the volume on the Gospels and Acts has magnificent illustrations, especially in Luke. *The Saint John's Bible: The Gospels and Acts.* (Collegeville, MN: Liturgical Press, 2005.)

• Notice that Jesus' whole sermon on Isaiah's text was just one sentence long! What is so promising about God's word in the Isaiah prophecy? What would people say if Jesus announced this message to your community, "Today it all happens!"?

3. Note the second half of the story when the people reject Jesus' message. After they said, "Is not this Joseph's son?" (4:22), Jesus apparently saw they had already rejected him and his mission from God. Read 4:23–27 carefully. What words or phrases seem to cause the crowd to turn angry? How would you feel if Jesus spoke like that in your congregation?

Historical Context

1. Luke's Gospel and the book of Acts give us rare glimpses into the synagogues of the first century. Historians and archeologists who study Jewish history have documented a wide variety of these local "houses of prayer" and "houses of study" from earlier centuries when the people of Israel were first "scattered" in Babylonia and Egypt (in the diaspora), and then through the times of the Greek and Roman Empires. While the temple was standing in Jerusalem, the synagogues in Judea and Galilee housed the local communities of faith for people in Judea and Galilee.

• Notice that Jesus "stood up to read" and "sat down" to speak. Imagine your church with no seating for the people. How would that feel different from most churches where preachers stand to speak while the people sit?

2. Imagine reading the book of Isaiah in the form of a scroll. The "book" with pages sewn together on a spine did not become standard until centuries after the time of Jesus. The synagogue in Nazareth probably owned hand-copied scrolls on sheepskin of the first five "books of Moses" (also known as the "law" or Torah) and of some prophets and writings. Those scrolls were treasures, probably kept in clay jars or secure wooden boxes.

• What if the pastor had to unroll a long scroll to find a passage from Isaiah? Would the scriptures seem more "holy" if they were on scrolls? How would that affect the way you'd listen if you couldn't read the Bible on your own?

• What if the only copies of the Bible were handwritten? Before the printing press and the Reformation, most people only heard the Bible read in worship, and often in Latin, which few people could understand. How do you experience the power of Isaiah's prophetic words when you hear them in the music of Handel's Messiah or as a direct address to you?

3. In Luke 4:19, Jesus is reading Isaiah's announcement of "the year of the Lord's favor." This is the "year of jubilee" and restoration promised in Leviticus 25:8–12. It meant debt forgiveness and restoration of land to those who had lost it in debt.

• Imagine a rural community where owning land is the economic backbone for families. Who would be glad and who would be unhappy if a "jubilee" were announced, giving land back to those whose property had been foreclosed?

Lutheran Context

1. The prophets knew that God had made their words "like a sharp sword" (Isaiah 49:2), cutting through human pretenses with both liberation for the oppressed and judgment on the oppressors. Luther emphasized that God's word communicates both God's commands and God's promises. God's law shines a light on our sins and self-interest just when we think we have hidden them in our achievements. Even God's promises disrupt the status quo, and we may be offended when we think we are entitled to our well-being. Such truth telling can also be "good news" for those who have been harmed by our self-righteousness.

• It is easy to criticize the people in Nazareth for rejecting Jesus, but what if you take Isaiah's promises literally, as personally addressed to you? Draw a picture of your face as you are hearing all of Jesus' words. You don't need to show the picture to anyone. When are you smiling and when are you wincing?

• How are Isaiah's words spoken by Jesus "good news" to you? Who might hear these words as the best news possible?

2. "Let God be God!" was one of the great watchwords of the Reformation, but that is not an easy instruction to follow. Most of the time, we are focused on our own schemes to get ahead and to be in control. Even congregations and denominations get stuck on achieving their own success when the world around them cries out in need. Jesus' sermon in Nazareth was and is a wake-up call to God's agenda for those in need.

 Tip:
A copy of Luther's translation of the Bible and a copy of the King James Version of the Bible could be displayed to remind people of the huge impact those Bibles made by getting the scriptures into the hands of the people and in their own languages. You might also encourage people to bring old family Bibles from their own ethnic pasts to help them grasp how "the first language of faith" (the Bible) has long been multilingual.

 Bonus Activity:
This would be a good session for someone to review the wonderful statement on the authority of the Word of God in the ELCA constitution (www.elca.org/What–We–Believe/Statements–of–Belief/ELCA–Confession–of–Faith.aspx). Remind the group about how Luther taught us to understand the word of God in these ways: in the scriptures, in our speaking of the gospel, and incarnate in Jesus Christ.

- Recall a time when your congregation paid more attention to people in need than to preserving itself. How was that experience threatening, and how was it liberating for the congregation?

Devotional Context

1. Look back to the Focus Image on page 19. What do you think is happening in the scene? How does the use of color affect the way you interpret this illustration? Have you ever had to speak to a hostile crowd? Have you ever had to take a stand for something against the majority? How is being a follower of Jesus sometimes a "minority" position?

2. Almost three centuries ago, Johannes Albrecht Bengel wrote:
> *"Apply yourself totally to the text.*
> *Apply the text totally to yourself."*

Understanding the Bible is the beginning of letting the word of Christ dwell in you richly (Colossians 3:16). Take time to dwell in this story, to savor, to appreciate, to meditate on the calling that God has for you as you follow Jesus in your home and family, your workplace, your public life, and your congregation. Write down some thoughts about this, and share them with another person in the group.

3. The bold vision for the Book of Faith initiative is:

That the whole church become more fluent in the first language of faith, the language of Scripture, in order that we might live into our calling as a people renewed, enlivened, empowered, and sent by the Word.

- Discuss this question with two other people: How does this story help you discern the calling and commission that God is giving your congregation, to be sent by Jesus into the world?

Wrap–up

1. If there are any questions to explore further, write them on chart paper or a whiteboard. Ask for volunteers to do further research to share with the group at the next session.

Bonus Activity:

Have learners consider writing or developing their personal mission statements. How do they see their own "mission in life" aligning with the mission Jesus lifts up in today's text? Ask learners to share their mission statements with one another.

Tip:

Lighting a candle in a dark or softly lit room during your opening or closing prayers may help people remember to welcome the presence of the living God. The Book of Faith initiative is not a scientific explanation.

Tip:

Ask the participants to look ahead to Luke 7:22–23 and read those verses aloud to them. Jesus quoted from Isaiah to announce what he was going to do, then he went about doing it. By chapter 7, which we will read for the next session, he called attention to what he was doing on the same terms as Isaiah's prophecy.

Pray

Almighty and ever-living God, increase in us the gifts of faith, hope, and love; and that we may obtain what you promise, make us love what you command, through your Son, Jesus Christ, our Savior and Lord. Amen.
(Collect for the fourth Sunday after Epiphany, ELW, p. 23)

Extending the Conversation (5 minutes)

Homework

1. Read the next session's Bible text: Luke 7:1–17.

2. Consider compiling a WWJD (What Would Jesus Do?) scrapbook. Week by week, as you are reading through Luke's Gospel, make clippings from the newspaper or magazines, insert photos from family and community events, and leave room for your own comments. In light of what Jesus said he was about to do and what he ultimately did in his mission, what would he do about these things?

3. Explore the Old Testament stories that Jesus refers to in today's text: Elijah in Sidon (1 Kings 17:1–16) and Elisha and the Syrian (2 Kings 5:1–14). Those stories provide biblical precedent for what Jesus does in Luke 7:1–17 (see the next session).

Enrichment

1. If you wish to read through the entire book of Luke during this unit, read the following sections this week:

  Day 1: Luke 4:31–44

  Day 2: Luke 5:1–11

  Day 3: Luke 5:12–26

  Day 4: Luke 5:27–39

  Day 5: Luke 6:1–11

  Day 6: Luke 6:12–19

  Day 7: Luke 6:20–49

2. Internet Web sites present varied interpretations of the year of Jubilee. Wikipedia can link you to both Jewish and Christian resources, such as Roman Catholic traditions of pilgrimage and several American Evangelical traditions of personal renewal.

Tip:
The closing prayer for this session is the prayer that is assigned for one of the Sundays in Advent when this passage from Luke 4 is the Gospel lesson. The first half of this story is read one week, and the second half is read one week later. The prayer alerts us to the fact that we are praying for divine help because, as Luther says in his explanation to the third article of the Apostles' Creed, "by our own reason or strength, we cannot believe in Jesus Christ or come to him."

Tip:
Encourage the participants to read the passages that are identified for "enrichment." Encourage them to read slowly, tracking how the story works.

For a "Jubilee" critique of the tyranny of debt in impoverished countries, see www.jubileeusa.org.

For Further Reading

The Gospel According to Luke by Michael F. Patella in New Collegeville Bible Commentary Series (Collegeville, MN: Liturgical Press, 2005), pp. 23–31.

"Session 3: Jesus Goes Public" in *Learning Luke: The Apostolic Gospel* by David L. Tiede and friends *(www.selectlearning.org)*.

Provoking the Gospel of Luke: A Storyteller's Commentary by Richard W. Swanson (Cleveland: Pilgrim Press, 2006), pp. 90–97.

Augsburg Commentary on the New Testament: Luke by David L. Tiede (Minneapolis: Augsburg Fortress, 1988), pp. 101–111.

Looking Ahead

1. Read the next session's Bible text: Luke 7:1–17.

2. Read through the Leader Guide for the next session and mark portions you wish to highlight for the group.

3. Make a checklist of any materials you'll need to do the Bonus Activities.

4. Pray for members of your group during the week.

5. Consult with the pastor or other congregational leaders about members of the congregation who are ill. The healing stories in Luke may cause distress about why they are not so quickly restored to health, as well as finding hope in seeing Jesus' care for afflicted people.

Luke 7:1–17

What Was Jesus Doing?

Leader Session Guide

Focus Statement

Jesus embodies God's authority and enacts God's compassion.

Key Verse

A great prophet has risen among us! God has looked favorably on his people!
Luke 7:16

Focus Image

The Sick Waiting for Jesus to Pass
James Tissot (1836–1902 French)
© SuperStock / SuperStock

Session Preparation

Before You Begin . . .

As you prepare to lead this session, pause to remember your own experiences with the illness or untimely death someone you love, perhaps your own times of illness. Jesus' dramatic actions in these stories are responses to human anguish, displaying God's compassion for those who suffer. Without promising that illness and death will all disappear, Jesus has given us glimpses of the world to come, disclosing that God empowers the vocations of all healers and helping us to anticipate the revelation of God's reign.

Session Instructions

1. Read this Session Guide completely and highlight or underline any portions you wish to emphasize with the group. Note any Bonus Activities you wish to do.

2. If you plan to do any special activities, check to see what materials you'll need, if any.

3. Have extra Bibles on hand in case a member of the group forgets to bring one.

4. Pay special attention to all who serve in the military or in medical vocations.

Session Overview

As God's messiah and prophet, Jesus went about Galilee, preaching, teaching, and healing. And he commissioned his disciples to continue these actions in his name. This session focuses on Jesus' raising the son of a widow and healing a **centurion**'s servant. The gospel does not promise that Jesus' followers will be immune to sickness and death, but Jesus provides glimpses of the life and healing that God intends for all who trust in God. These stories empower the vocations of all healers and heralds of life beyond death.

LITERARY CONTEXT

Enacting the script he announced in Nazareth (see the previous session on Luke 4:14–30), Jesus is actually doing what he said the Messiah would do. Like a true prophet (see Deuteronomy 18:22), Jesus demonstrates the truth of his words through his actions. In a few verses after these stories, when questions are asked of him by

? Centurion:

A centurion had charge over one hundred soldiers in the Roman army. During the Roman occupation of Galilee and Judea, Roman troops were garrisoned in major cities like Caesarea and Jerusalem to enforce the Roman order.

disciples of John the Baptist (7:20), Jesus will respond about who he truly is in God's scheme of things. His comments point back to the Messiah's agenda he announced in Luke 4: "Go and tell John what you have seen and heard: the blind receive their sight, the lame walk, the lepers are cleansed, the deaf hear, the dead are raised, the poor have good news brought to them" (Luke 7:22).

The activity suggestions in the literary section in the Learner Session Guide are focused on (a) the centurion's recognition of Jesus' authority and (b) Jesus' breaking of the protocol for Jewish funerals, because as Messiah, he has the command of both life and death. For the first suggestion, look for some experience in which the "chain of command" was pre-empted by a "higher power" or a critical intelligence from outside the system. A good example is the old story of the captain of the battleship who altered his course when a junior officer radioed in to tell him that the captain's command of the sea would not allow him to challenge the rocky reefs on which the lighthouse stood in darkness.

The second suggestion moves toward appreciating the personal impact of God's presence. Sometimes, people don't pay much attention when they say, "Oh my God!" or even "Thank God!" But what if it is true that you sensed God's presence or were blessed by God? Then how would your story be affected by God and God's purposes? When God comes into our lives, invited or not, how dare we return to "business as usual" as if there were no God and as if God had not called us to become a blessing to others.

? Jewish Elders:

The Jewish elders were probably local synagogue officials. We can only guess about how they felt to be sent to Jesus on this assignment from a Roman centurion.

HISTORICAL CONTEXT

In Jesus' era, the Jewish people were already deeply divided by the Roman occupation. The Romans brought the peace of stability, even prosperity to a privileged few. Some Romans were respectful, even awed by the faith of Israel. Others were cynical and coercive, as we will see in Pontius Pilate's behavior during Jesus' trial. Under the yoke of heavy taxation and strict Roman rulers, many Jews "went along to get along," but some fomented revolt, and others tried to stand apart. The **Jewish elders**—who were sent by the centurion to tell Jesus that the centurion was "worthy" to have his servant healed—risked being criticized by other Jews as "collaborators with the Romans." Jesus even appeared to be surprised by the faith he found in this Gentile Roman officer. Jesus' mission was to Israel (Luke 4:43-44), but this encounter anticipates God's mission to the nations.

A few decades later in Luke's time, the followers of Jesus had expanded Jesus' mission among the Jewish communities—scattered throughout the empire—with the message that Jesus, the Messiah of Israel, is also the Savior of the world. Once the Romans had crushed Israel and destroyed the temple about forty year after Jesus' death and resurrection, this appeal by Jesus' followers beyond the Jewish community gained new strength in the empire. But the Christian mission to go "to the ends of the earth" also offended those Jews who believed that Israel's hope lay in more strict observance of the law, not in gathering non-Jews into God's reign.

The first activity proposed in the Learner Session Guide seeks to help people understand the surprise (or maybe even the offense) they feel when "those people" whom "we" regard as "outsiders" receive the good news of the gospel. In Luke's story about Peter, the apostle communicated that same shock when he declared, "Who was I that I could hinder God?" (Acts 11:17). As it turns out, evangelism is not about making everybody like us. We are turned toward God ourselves (being converted) as God opens the door to all tribes and people.

The second activity seeks to explore Jesus' compassion as a revealing of the heart of God. Jesus practiced "messianic license," taking the freedom that comes with the authority of being the Messiah. But that was not his personal whim. It was a revelation of how God's heart was touched by the suffering of the widow. So forget propriety! Her need had priority!

The freedom to act on behalf of those in need is one of the great powers of the gospel. We know it when we see it. Sometimes, the most unlikely people exercise this freedom. They are the people who don't wait for permission to break the rules for the sake of serving others. Somehow, they know that forgiveness, even for disruptive acts of compassion, will come from God. If their authority to act with this freedom of compassion comes from Jesus, all the better!

Lutheran Context

The Book of Faith Initiative belongs in a long history of Lutheran efforts to help the people of God to read the Bible. Some participants may have experienced other programs as well, such as The Bethel Bible Series, Word and Witness, Crossways, or Search. All of those initiatives are grounded in excellent biblical scholarship and confidence that the whole Bible—Old Testament and New Testament together—brings us into the presence of the living God.

The story of Jesus' raising the widow's son illustrates the comparison that Martin Luther once made between the Bible and a great river: a child can play safely in its shallows and an elephant could drown in its depths. Any child can sense God's great power at work through Jesus' compassion, and the story only gets richer and deeper when the scriptural precedents from the Elijah and Elisha narratives are explored in 1 Kings and 2 Kings, respectively. We can't read Jesus' mind, but we can see that he was re-enacting the prophetic demonstrations of God's care and deliverance. When the evangelist uses the simple phrase about Jesus ("He gave the widow's son to his mother"), the words are an exact quote from the Elijah story in 1 Kings 17:23.

Lutherans know that we are not the first or last to read the Bible faithfully. In fact, with all people of good will, we are eager to read the Bible together to hear what others see and understand from it. But as we dwell in the scriptures as the "first language of faith," we discover that the Bible also "reads" or "interprets" our lives. That is the insight in the traditional Lutheran view of the Bible as the "mirror" that illuminates our lives.

Jesus was enacting the script of the prophetic drama, the evangelist was interpreting Jesus' actions in light of Israel's scriptures, and our eyes are now open to see God's compassion at work in all kinds of human acts of care and healing. Scripture interprets scripture, and scripture interprets life as lived in the presence of God.

As practical people who were readers of the Bible, Lutherans who immigrated to North America quickly got to the business of building orphanages, hospitals, and chaplaincies. They also founded seminaries and colleges at a scale far exceeding their numbers, but these stories about the centurion and the widow direct our attention primarily to why Lutherans established ministries of compassion and healing for others (and not just for ourselves). God's script was old as Elijah and Elisha, enacted by Jesus, and empowered by the Spirit. As those saved by faith in Christ Jesus, this was just how you acted in good faith.

DEVOTIONAL CONTEXT

Saving faith is more than right belief. It is a matter of the heart and the will (which is generally even more stubborn than the mind). The centurion's recognition that he was not "worthy" of having Jesus come under his roof was coupled with his unqualified confidence that Jesus only had to say the word for the centurion's servant to be healed. Somehow, only by the miracle of faith, the centurion got to the level at which trust lies: in the heart. Maybe the elders already saw that in him because they identified him by saying that he is "someone who loves our people." Clearly, Jesus believed in the centurion's military comment about authority systems as clear evidence of his implicit trust. "I tell you, not even in Israel have I found such faith."

This session offers an excellent opportunity to explore what it means to be "worthy" in the presence of God. The centurion wasn't all knotted up with guilt, but he was awed by Jesus' divine authority and knew that Jesus was out of his league. It is important to note that Jesus did not insist that the centurion humble himself further. Mere mortal sinners as we are, we have learned to come to the Lord's table with the centurion's prayer, "Lord, I am not worthy that I could come into your presence. Only say the word and I will be whole."

We are not groveling, but we are made worthy in our deep dependence on God's mercy. Our hope for healing in body and soul is anchored in our confidence in God's compassion. Our salvation comes not by "any merit or worthiness in [us]" but in our trusting God's grace.

This session also opens the worlds of human vocations in compassion and healing. The Greek word that expresses Jesus' "compassion" is literally visceral: "he was touched in his intestines." Compassion means "suffering with," and when humans are deeply moved by grief or joy, they feel it in their "guts." If all of this talk of body parts sounds gross to us, imagine how offensive it was to the Greeks who thought that being a god meant being "above it all," never suffering any mortal pains.

Christian vocations in compassion and healing are grounded in the incarnation itself, the theology of the cross where God meets us in the depth of our suffering. Ministries of compassion continue to be callings into uncomfortable places, like mortuaries where bodies must be buried or cremated and messy field hospitals where blood is spilled. Those who empty bedpans and perform autopsies need to be encouraged that theirs are not merely dirty jobs that someone must do. Through their work, they are enacting God's compassion.

The devotional dimensions of these stories are alive to our saving trust in God's love for us and empowered by our vocations to enact God's compassion for our neighbors.

Facilitator's Prayer

Lord Jesus, we are now following you as you publicly display your authority as God's Messiah and reveal the depth of your compassion. Open our minds and our hearts to see and to hear God at work in you and for us. May we join the crowds in glorifying God, who has visited our human realm in you and dignified our lives with your compassion. May my leadership of this session serve to strengthen the participants' trust in you and empower their callings in the world you love. In your name, I pray. Amen.

Gather (10–15 minutes)

Check–in

Invite learners to share completed homework or any new thoughts or insights about the previous session. Be ready to give a brief recap of that session if necessary.

Pray

Almighty God, you inspired your servant Luke to reveal in his gospel the love and healing power of your Son. Give your church the same love and power to heal, and to proclaim your salvation among the nations to the glory of your name, through Jesus Christ, your Son, our healer, who lives and reigns with you and the Holy Spirit, one God, now and forever. Amen.
(Collect for the day of Luke, Evangelist, October 18, ELW, p. 58)

Focus Activity

Look at the Focus Image titled The Sick Waiting for Jesus to Pass. What kinds of illnesses or physical challenges do you imagine some of the people by the road are experiencing? Have you or someone close to you ever waited for, hoped for healing? Are you or this other person still waiting?

Tip:
Supplying every person with the name and/or picture of someone who is ill or has recently died is just one way to encourage participants to sense how the Gospel stories shed light on our lives.

Tip:
Encourage people to notice how the prayers for each Sunday are almost always linked with the Gospel lesson.

Tip:
Along with the Focus Activity, a few minutes of silent prayer can help people to calm the frenzy of their lives as they call upon the compassion of the living God for someone in need.

In the story of the centurion, the officer interceded for his servant. In the story of the widow of Nain, Jesus was deeply moved by the death of the widow's son. Knowing our Lord's compassion for all who suffer and confident in the great resurrection of all who belong to Christ Jesus, pray now for God's healing and love for someone who is ill or in need of comfort.

Open Scripture (10–15 minutes)

If you have a military officer (active or retired) and a health professional in a field related to health or death and dying in your group, consider asking the officer to read the first story of the centurion to the participants and the health professional to read the story of the widow's son.

Or you could ask a volunteer to be the narrator, reading all but the speaking verses. Then you could ask two or three men to read the Jewish elders' lines in verses 4–5 and 2–3 women to read the lines of the centurion's friends in verses 6b–8. Another man or woman could read Jesus' words in verses 9, 1.

Read Luke 7:1–17.
- What images in these stories of healing stand out to you? Why?
- What questions do these stories raise as you listen to them?
- With which character do you most closely identify?

Join the Conversation (25–55 minutes)

Literary Context

1. The story of the healing of the centurion's servant follows Jesus' "Sermon on the Plain" (6:17–49), and Luke introduces a new section of the narrative by reporting that "after Jesus had finished all his sayings he entered Capernaum" (7:1). The Messiah has been announcing his program, and now he will show his prophetic compassion as Messiah. In this part of the story, Jesus will be well-received and will not encounter rejection.

- In the first scene, notice the relationship between the Jewish elders and the Roman centurion. What surprising thing has the centurion done for his Jewish neighbors?
- The centurion displays what military personnel call "the habit of command." He knows how to give orders and he knows when

Tip:

You might introduce the story by reminding people of how the narrative is unfolding. You could mention that Jesus is enacting the program he announced in Nazareth. He has just concluded his Sermon on the Plain (Luke 6:17–49). Soon, in his response to questions from John's disciples (Luke 7:22), Jesus will recap what he has been doing.

Bonus Activity:

Make up a skit to show how surprised and impressed the people probably were when the Roman centurion identified Jesus' authority as superior to his.

Tip:

You might consider exploring these stories in parallel columns in a book called a "Gospel Parallel" or a "Synopsis of the Gospels." The word "synopsis" means to "see things together," and since the early church, the first three Gospels have often been studied in parallel columns. Most scholars conclude that Luke and Matthew used a version of Mark's Gospel as the basis for their accounts and that they also had another source. That additional source has been called "Q" because the German word for "source" is Quelle. It is believed that this story of the centurion was edited from that source by both Matthew and Luke.

Tip:

Provide paper and colored pencils or markers.

Bonus Activity:

This could be a good occasion for someone to investigate the peril of poverty and the loss of standing in the community that a woman in Jesus' time faced after her husband and her son(s) had died. Good Bible dictionaries will include an article on widows.

---

he is outranked. How does that come out when Jesus comes near to the centurion's house? What is Jesus' reaction?

2. Compare this story in Luke's Gospel to Matthew's version (see Matthew 8:5–13). What differences do you see? What role does faith play in each?

3. Jesus' compassion for the widow reveals him to be a Messiah with heart. Notice how he breaks into the funeral and crosses the boundaries of clean and unclean by walking up and touching the cot on which they were carrying the corpse. Tell a story of a time when you have seen a person of authority set it all aside because he or she was moved by someone's suffering.

4. In Luke's narrative, the message that God will "visit [God's] people" (or as it is translated in the NRSV, "look favorably on [God's] people") is sounded hopefully in Zechariah's song in Luke 1:68, and later resounds with Jesus' judgment as he approached Jerusalem ("because you did not recognize the time of your visitation from God." Luke 19:44).

- Recall a time when you were aware that God was with you to protect, heal, or guide you. Something more than good luck was with you. Maybe like the people in Nain, you even said (aloud or under your breath), "Thank God!" In the story of your life, what did you do next?

Historical Context

1. The centurion was an officer in the army of Roman occupation. Like the centurion in a different story whom Peter visited when directed by a heavenly vision (Acts 10:1–48), this officer was not an Israelite but was known as a friend of Israel. Many parts of Luke's gospel involve outsiders who are more faithful than the insiders.

- Draw a picture of someone you know or know about who understood Jesus and his mission when people inside the church lagged behind.

- Watch the newspaper for a story of military service personnel who show forth the love of Christ in places where nationals resent them as occupiers.

2. Jewish tradition has long been very careful about burial practices, and Christians have continued that respect. Biblical faith, however, knows a power greater than death. In Nain, Jesus enacted the prophetic faith that God's love is stronger than death.

- Many people grieve their sons and daughters who have gone to early graves because of accidents, violence, or disease. Jesus doesn't interrupt those services. How does this story help you envision Jesus' authority, even over death?

Lutheran Context

1. One of the deep Lutheran convictions about the Bible is that scripture itself often gives the best interpretation of scripture because it is all God's story and action. That is why we also read scripture as a mirror to make sense of our own lives. Sometimes, interpretation of scripture by the scripture happens directly, as when Jesus declared Isaiah's prophecy as fulfilled in Nazareth (Luke 4:21) and where he cited the prophetic precedents of Elijah and Elisha in Luke 4:25–27. But Jesus often enacted or re-enacted God's story in scripture without specifically saying it.

Jesus' healing of the centurion's son reminds us of Elisha's healing of the foreign army commander Naaman in 2 Kings (5:1–19), and Jesus' raising in Nain is almost a replay of Elijah's raising of a widow's son in 1 Kings (17:17–24).

- Compare the stories from 1 Kings and 2 Kings with the stories in today's text from Luke. How do those Old Testament stories help shed light on the meaning of the New Testament stories in Luke? How is God at work in each?

2. Both stories from the Old Testament conclude when the great prophet "gave him to his mother." That is not mere coincidence or an accident of history, because God who has long been full of compassion for widows and orphans is still at work.

- Take time to listen to one another. Who has experienced this kind of divine care in a time of need? What stories have you heard about such love from God? How does reading these Bible stories help you to sense God among us?

3. Maybe some of those in great need around you are actually widows or parents who have lost children. Maybe you know young people who have been lost to drugs or prostitution. Take some time with local school personnel, police, and social service agencies to identify who is at the greatest risk in your community. Then ask yourself, "What was Jesus doing with the widow and her son? What would Jesus do now, and for whom?"

Tip:

Notice that this session alerts you to both Lutheran theology and Lutheran vocations in human services.

Bonus Activity:

Encourage participants to read the old prophetic stories of Elijah and Elisha in 1 Kings 17 and 2 Kings 5, respectively. As Jesus announced in Luke 4:14–30, the coming of God's prophet brought blessings to those inside and outside of Israel who had the faith to trust what God was doing. The prophets, however, also provoked rejection from those who did not receive them as coming from God.

Bonus Activity:

If someone shows interest in the military, this would be an opportunity to direct him or her to the ELCA Web site (elca.org) to find out about the church's work in military chaplaincy. This ministry of the whole church has a long and distinguished history in which Lutherans have demonstrated leadership throughout the twentieth century.

Tip:

Evangelical Lutheran Worship has many fine prayers and several hymns related to healing. Note, for example, "Healer of Our Every Ill" (ELW 612).

Bonus Activity:

Ask a good singer to lead you in singing the gospel canticle for morning on page 303 of ELW, read the words of the canticle or as a group. These words come directly from Zechariah's canticle in Luke 1, and they are wonderful interpretations of our stories. Pay particular attention to verses 7-10 where Jesus' role as "the prophet of the Most High" is described.

Tip:

We are bold to call on God's compassion, not because our faith will control what God does, but because Jesus has given us confidence to trust God's love to be with us.

Devotional Context

1. These two stories offer glimpses of God's compassion. The prophets of Israel were swept into the anguish of God's love. The God of the Bible is not detached or living in the clouds. Biblical prophecy is alive with divine pathos. In Jesus, God came to earth, touched by human suffering and pained by human indifference.

- What words do you think Jesus the Messiah has for those who do not experience physical healing in response to their prayers for help?
- How do you see the stories of Jesus the Healer as both promising and potentially painful?

2. Draw one picture of Jesus healing the servant of this foreign soldier and another picture of him taking on death itself on behalf of the widow. If possible, draw the faces of participants in this study on the crowds of amazed people as they declare: "A great prophet has risen among us! God has looked favorably on his people" (Luke 7:16).

3. Sometimes, we do not ask for healing help because we feel unworthy to receive it. What would it take for you to feel "worthy" to have Jesus come to your aid?

4. What would it mean for Jesus to "visit" your congregation? What healing do you hope he would bring?

Wrap-up

1. If there are any questions to explore further, write them on chart paper or a whiteboard. Ask for volunteers to do further research to share with the group at the next session.

2. Jesus shows God's care for our lives and our health here and now, not only in heaven. How do these stories of Jesus' compassion give you courage? How does God's compassion give you hope when your physical malady may or may not be cured?

Pray

Come, Lord Jesus, be our guest,
And may the world you love be blessed.
Messiah and Prophet of compassion,
Draw near to us and us to you,
That we may live your resurrection. Amen.

Extending the Conversation (5 minutes)

Homework

1. Read the next session's Bible text: Luke 9:18–36.

2. Visit someone who is homebound or in the hospital. Find out if the individual knows that people are praying for him or her. Invite that person to tell you how he or she remains confident that God is with him or her, even at times when friends and family are not present.

3. Call the family of someone in your community who is serving in the military. Let the family know that they have your prayerful support, and ask for a photo of their loved one so that you can pray for that person by name. Reach out in this way to more than one family, if possible.

Enrichment

1. If you wish to read through the entire book of Luke during this unit, read the following sections this week:

Day 1: Luke 7:18–35
Day 2: Luke 7:36–50
Day 3: Luke 8:1–18
Day 4: Luke 8:19–25
Day 5: Luke 8:26–39
Day 6: Luke 8:40–56
Day 7: Luke 9: 1–17

2. Lutheran Services in America is an umbrella organization for a wide variety of Lutheran social ministries. From the time of the immigration of Lutherans into North America through the eras of relocating refugees after every war, Lutherans have simply known that God has called us to serve our neighbors, whether they are Lutheran or Christian or not. In the past two centuries, Lutherans have developed the largest faith-based network of social ministries in North America. Visit the Web site of Lutheran Services in America to report on the range and complexity of this work. Serving our neighbors started with Jesus in stories like those in chapter 7 of Luke.

3. Lutherans have also been industry leaders in the development of hospital and medical care for disease and trauma. The economics and public policies of twenty-first century health care have made it more difficult to sustain the Christian identity of hospital systems that were once vigorously Lutheran. Still, almost every community and congregation includes people whose occupations in health care are profound vocations for them. If your congregation has a parish nurse or includes physicians or other health care providers, ask one of the learners to interview one of those professionals to explore this question: "How is your work a fulfillment of Jesus' ministry of healing?"

For Further Reading

The Gospel According to Luke by Michael F. Patella in New Collegeville Bible Commentary Series (Collegeville, MN: Liturgical Press, 2005), pp. 47–50.

"Session 4: Messiah and Prophet" in *Learning Luke: The Apostolic Gospel* with David L. Tiede and friends (www.selectlearning.org).

Provoking the Gospel of Luke: A Storyteller's Commentary by Richard W. Swanson (Cleveland: Pilgrim Press, 2006).

Augsburg Commentary on the New Testament: Luke by David L. Tiede (Minneapolis: Augsburg Fortress, 1988), pp. 147–159.

Looking Ahead

1. Read the next session's Bible text: Luke 9:18–36.

2. Read through the Leader Guide for the next session and mark portions you wish to highlight for the group.

3. Make a checklist of any materials you'll need to do the Bonus Activities.

4. Pray for members of your group during the week.

Luke 9:18–36

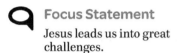
Leader Session Guide

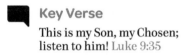
Focus Statement

Jesus leads us into great challenges.

Key Verse

This is my Son, my Chosen; listen to him! Luke 9:35

Focus Image

© Flirt / SuperStock

Why Must Jesus Die?

Session Preparation

Before You Begin . . .

This session will take you up into the glory and deep into the struggle of Jesus' mission. Allow yourself to be honest about how much you prefer the glorious revelation of who Jesus is compared to the difficult truth that his mission of love will take him into harm's way. It is easier—or at least it seems to be easier—to adore Jesus on the mountaintop than to follow him on his passionate journey where the forces will be aligned against him. Yet this is the pathway of God's love, moving into the world for those who need it most.

Session Instructions

1. Read this Session Guide completely and highlight or underline any portions you wish to emphasize with the group. Note any Bonus Activities you wish to do.

2. If you plan to do any bonus activities, check to see what materials you'll need, if any.

3. Have extra Bibles on hand in case a member of the group forgets to bring one.

Session Overview

The verses from Luke in this session are filled with the great variety of names, titles, and identities that people used for Jesus, including what he called himself (**Son of Man**) and how God identified him (**my Son, my Chosen**). All of those titles give valuable clues that Jesus was understood to be the fulfillment of God's promises to Israel, each one answering in scriptural terms, "Who is Jesus?" But as we get all of those titles straight, the enduring question becomes "Why did Jesus have to die?"

LITERARY CONTEXT

In your preparation to lead this session, take time to read the stories that precede and follow our verses, paying special attention to the verses that are mentioned in the Learner Session Guide. Luke's narrative highlights how Jesus is now preparing his disciples (the **twelve** in Luke 9:1–6 and the **seventy** in Luke 10:1–12) to represent his mission with very specific instructions. This is the authorization that Jesus' disciples (learners) receive as they become apostles (sent ones). Then we glimpse Jesus' firm,

? Son of Man:

A scriptural term that can mean simply a "human being," as when God sends the mere mortal Ezekiel (2:1–8) on a mission to deliver prophetic words of judgment. In Daniel 7:13, however, the "Son of Man" remains a human figure, but one who comes on the clouds of heaven to bring God's final judgment on the nations. In using the term for himself, therefore, Jesus is claiming prophetic authority, at the very least, and he may already be suggesting his role at God's right hand in the last judgment.

? My Son, My Chosen:

The voice from heaven also identified Jesus as "My Son" when he was anointed "Messiah/Christ" by the Holy Spirit in his baptism. This is the language of kingship in Israel, where, just as in Psalm 2, the king was anointed as God's son, that is, a human "messiah". Later in Christian history, when Jesus was called "God's Son," the emphasis was on his divinity, but Luke's story is focused on Jesus' identity as Israel's king of God's own choosing.

When the voice from heaven calls Jesus "My Chosen," its immediate meaning is that this is the king whom God selected. But the word "chosen" is also filled with prophetic meaning from Isaiah (42:1–4), or, what it means to be chosen as the servant who suffers. Only Luke (23:35) uses this term as one that is on the lips of those who are deriding Jesus on the cross.

? The Twelve:

They are identified in Luke 22:30 as those who will judge the twelve tribes of Israel. After Judas' betrayal of Christ, the full number was restored in Acts 1:12–26 before the coming of the Holy Spirit at Pentecost.

? The Seventy:

In some texts, the number is "seventy-two." This number apparently reflects the seventy elders chosen by Moses from the twelve tribes (Exodus 24:1, 9; Numbers 11:16,24) or the nations in Genesis 10.

prophetic intention, knowing that the opposition to Jesus will become fierce (Luke 9:51–53; 13:31–33).

The first section of the Learner Session Guide focuses on discipleship. Jesus' call to follow him is both uncompromising and joy-filled. The joy is experienced in the glory of Jesus as God's Son and Chosen One, but God's ways are not our ways. Thus, following Jesus proves to be a dangerous—even deathly—pathway because the forces that stand against Jesus and his reign are unyielding. Only Jesus' promise endures beyond inevitable rejection: "Those who lose their life for my sake will save it" (Luke 9:24).

Maybe a participant knows of someone who has refused to "go along with the crowd," even when that decision put his or her future (or even life) at risk. Consider the bumper sticker with this question: "If you were on trial for being Jesus' disciple, would there be any evidence to convict you?"

The second section of the Learner Guide takes us deeper into the "liberation" or "salvation" that Jesus is performing. He is not a suicidal radical rushing to his death. He is on God's mission to accomplish a new **exodus,** or rescue. Jesus is intense and passionate, filled with God's compassionate love—no matter what comes!

Time and again when a child falls into a swirling river, the little one's mother or father dives in without thinking twice. Offering that kind of self-giving love goes deeper than being sensible. Ask your group to explore this love, this compassion. How far would they go to rescue their children, grandchildren, nieces, or nephews whose lives are at risk?

HISTORICAL CONTEXT

Several decades after the events took place, Luke is telling what happened to Jesus and affirms that Jesus was no victim of fate or politics. Jesus was driving the action forward. He was enacting God's script.

Note Herod's perplexed comments in Luke 9:7–9. Since the time that he executed John the Baptist (Luke 3:19–20; 7:27), Herod became distressed even by rumors that John was back or that Elijah had now come as promised by the prophets (Malachi 4:5). Herod will again threaten Jesus (13:31) and play an evil role in Jesus' trial (23:6–12).

Tyrants—such as Hitler, Stalin, or Osama bin Laden slaughter innocent people, sometimes in service of a grandiose ideology or even in the name of God. How does Jesus' death in the midst of evil strengthen those who suffer? Talk with participants to make a list of Christian martyrs who have given their lives in witness to Jesus' reign of mercy and justice.

LUTHERAN CONTEXT

Martin Luther's strong affirmation of the "theology of the cross" was never a glorification of suffering (as if to say that we could earn our salvation by being victims). Theology is first about God, and the gospel has God as the actor, or subject, of the action. Thus the "theology of the cross" is first about how God accomplished our liberation, or salvation, through Jesus' crucifixion and resurrection.

Jesus did not die on a church altar between two candles, but on an executioner's hill outside the city walls of Jerusalem, crucified by Pontius Pilate. How does Jesus' deeply human suffering touch your life with God's compassion?

People have many kinds of religious experiences, sometimes associated with dreams or the visions of death or near-death experiences. In the time of the early Christians, the **Gnostics** were fascinated with Moses, Elijah, and Enoch, because they had unusual "departures" from the earth. But Luke's stories of Moses, Elijah, and Jesus help us recognize where the God of the Bible comes down to earth in our various experiences. No one controls or possesses God, but God calls and sends people in both ordinary and dramatic ways.

Consider this question: How does God speak to you when God's voice from the cloud tells the disciples, "This is my Son, my Chosen; listen to him!"

DEVOTIONAL CONTEXT

This session provides an excellent opportunity to explore several of the powerful titles that are used for Jesus. Consider how each of them might have carried great meaning with the people of Israel who were hoping for God's redemption. Then pay attention to how the meaning of those glorious titles is affected by the fact that Jesus brought each one of them "down to earth." Give thanks to God for Jesus, who is God's way of ruling the world!

 Exodus:

Moses led the Israelites out of Egypt. At the time of Jesus, Moses and the prophet Elijah were understood never to have died and never to have been buried, so that they could reenter human history as representatives of God's interests.

Gnostics (pronounced "NAH–sticks"):

This term was used for those who were caught up in exploring secret knowledge (*gnosis*) or divine mysteries of spiritual realities. Some Jews and Christians were deeply influenced by Jesus' teachings that conveyed higher knowledge or spiritual wisdom. To this day, Jesus appeals to some people more as a guru of wisdom to transport us above than for inaugurating God's kingdom on earth.

Dietrich Bonhoeffer was a Lutheran pastor and theologian who was executed for participating in a plot on Hitler's life. In his book *Discipleship*, Bonhoeffer wrote:

> Whenever Christ calls us, his call leads us to death. Whether we, like the first disciples, must leave house and vocation to follow him, or whether, with Luther, we leave the monastery for a secular vocation, in both cases the same death awaits us, namely, death in Jesus Christ, the death of our old self caused by the call of Jesus.... As Christ bears our burdens, so we are to bear the burden of our sisters and brothers.... Jesus' call to bear the cross places all who follow him in the community of the forgiveness of sins. (Translated by Barbara Green and Reinhard Krauss. Minneapolis: Fortress Press, 2001, pp. 87–88).

Explore with the learners what it means to be "chosen" by God. What is threatening or scary about that? What is life-giving and hopeful about it? Discuss what Jesus' experience means for life in the real world. For example, Martin Luther King's speeches were filled with the reality of a life in danger. He knew he might die before his dreams were fully realized. How does faith or living for a particular purpose give us strength to endure hardship and even death?

Facilitator's Prayer

Lord Jesus Christ, you have come among us in the splendor of God's mercy. We are awed at God's power working through you to accomplish our salvation, liberating us from sin, death, and the power of evil. We are humbled to learn how costly this mission of God's compassion was for you and continues to be for us as your followers. Still, we pray for God's kingdom of justice and mercy to come among us. Abide with us, Lord Jesus, that we may follow you in life and in death, trusting in your love. Amen.

Gather (10–15 minutes)

Check-in

Invite learners to share completed homework or any new thoughts or insights about the previous session. Be ready to give a brief recap of that session if necessary.

 Tip:
Encourage the participants to take time to appreciate the daily readings. The story is now leading us along Jesus' pathway as he demonstrates his authority and encounters opposition. The story is simple, but mature experience will appreciate its depth.

Pray

Lord Jesus, you have called us to follow you as your disciples, and you have sent us into the world to be your apostles among all those people you love, even those who despise you. You never promised it would be easy, but you went before us with courage, vision, and determination, even to your death, which you saw coming. We pray today to be caught up in your mission, unafraid to follow you and confident of your love for us. Amen.

Focus Activity

Take a close look at the Focus Image. What do you imagine has happened/is happening? What do you think the rescuer is feeling? Have you ever been in a desperate rescue situation, either as the one being rescued or as the one doing the rescuing? Do you know someone whose work involves serving in dangerous situations?

Tip:

Encourage learners to settle themselves, allow for silence, and pray slowly without anxiety. As his life is on the line, Jesus' mission is now drawing us deeper into our callings as disciples.

Open Scripture (10–15 minutes)

If one reader volunteers to read through all of these verses, take some time preparing the reader to feel the breaks after verses 20, 22, and 27, then to continue as a complete narrative through verses 28–36. The reading should be done slowly, allowing Jesus' hard words and the disciples' lack of understanding to be heard.

An alternative would be to assign a narrator to read all the portions that are not quotations. The whole group could be the crowd in verse 19, and a single reader could speak Jesus' words in 18, 20 (first half), and 23–27. Another voice could speak for Peter in verses 20 (second half) and 33, and one more could speak. And one more could speak from the cloud in verse 35.

Read Luke 9:18–36.
- What words or actions caught your attention in these verses?
- How do Jesus' words about following him make you feel?
- What was most awesome to you about Jesus' transfiguration?

Bonus Activity:

Invite someone from the community who has shown the deep courage of faith to tell his or her story. This could be someone who endured a long illness in the confidence that God was with him or her, or an emergency worker who has served in dangerous places with the awareness that this is just what Jesus' followers do. Don't make the visitor into a hero, but welcome that person as a disciple who can tell about how God was always there during hard times.

Tip:

Allow time for silence as you read each of the three questions stated in the Learner Session Guide. Be especially slow with the second question about how Jesus' words make the participants feel. If no one responds, let it rest. Silence doesn't mean they missed the question.

Tip:

When you ask the question, "Why must Jesus die?" don't settle for the "right answer" that some may offer. Keep the question alive so that all of you may be drawn deeply into the mystery of God's compassion for real people in the real world.

Bonus Activity:

Notice that the stories in our session are sandwiched between the sending of the twelve and the sending of the seventy. Set up a "recruitment desk" with a line for "the twelve" and a line on the other side for "the seventy." Next, post recruitment messages from Jesus for each group. Examples can include selections from Luke 9:1–6 and Luke 10:3–11. Over the recruitment desk, write "If any want to become my followers, let them deny themselves and take up their crosses daily and follow me." Then ask the whole group two questions:

1. Why does Jesus have more followers than any other person in human history?

2. Why would you sign up to be one of the twelve or one of the seventy?

Join the Conversation (25–55 minutes)

Literary Context

We are at the point in the story when Jesus is completing a major phase of teaching, with demonstrations of who he is as Messiah and Prophet of God. Shortly after the end of our reading for this session, Jesus will "set his face to go to Jerusalem," and the Samaritans will not receive him "because his face was set toward Jerusalem" (9:51–53).

The question "Who is Jesus?" leads us with Jesus' disciples to other questions that fill us with concern: "Who are we?" "What does it mean to follow Jesus?" We are drawn into the story with both hope and fear. In the light of Jesus' transfiguration, we sense that Jesus is on a path to unavoidable conflict, suffering, and death. Why must Jesus die? Our fear, "What will become of us?" is illumined by our faith that through difficulties and even death, God's reign is coming. As Paul and Barnabas later encouraged the disciples in Antioch, "It is through many persecutions that we must enter the kingdom of God" (Acts 14:22).

1. Our story follows Jesus' authorization of the mission of the twelve disciples and the intimidating question from Herod, who asks, "Who is this about whom I hear such things?" Read Luke 9:1–6 and Luke 9:7–9.

• Compare the sending of the twelve in Luke 9:1–6 with the sending of the seventy in 10:1–12. How are the disciples told to travel? The ancient world was well acquainted with traveling hucksters and religious scams. When have you seen someone representing Jesus with the integrity of simplicity?

2. Peek ahead to Luke 13:31–33 to see how Herod's threat escalates to the point that he wants to kill Jesus. Herod will appear again in Jesus' trial in Jerusalem. Think of one or more other tyrants who first became an adversary and then the executioner of a righteous person. Why did that person take that path?

3. The glory of God shines forth with words of acclamation for Jesus from the cloud. This story is told in close agreement with Mark 9:2–10 and Matthew 17:1–9, but only Luke includes the rich details about how Moses and Elijah were "speaking of [Jesus'] departure, which he was about to accomplish in Jerusalem" (Luke 9:31–33). The Greek word for "departure" is *exodus*, like the name of the Old Testament book of Exodus that tells the story of Israel's miraculous departure, or exodus, from Egypt.

• Imagine how the message of Jesus' accomplishing a departure/ exodus would have sounded to Simeon and Anna who were "looking forward to the consolation of Israel" and "looking for the redemption of Jerusalem" (Luke 2:25,38). Can you feel the hope growing even as the threat rises?

4. The story of the Transfiguration is the concluding Gospel lesson in the Epiphany season of the church year, and it is followed by Ash Wednesday and Lent. Many readers have sensed that this story is a preview of the accounts of Jesus' resurrection. The concluding sentence reads: "And they kept silent and in those days told no one any of the things they had seen" (Luke 9:36).

• Why do you think the disciples chose to be silent about this experience? In what way do you consider the transfiguration and resurrection of Jesus to be similar?

Historical Context

As we hear "the greatest story ever told" about Jesus' ministry and mission, we need to remember that the evangelists wrote about events that actually happened. Writing forty to fifty years after Jesus' life, death, and resurrection, they were retelling the stories that "eyewitnesses and servants of the word" (Luke 1:2) had chosen to tell in both oral and written forms. They had seen God's Messiah at work. At this point in Luke's account, the disciples see God at work in Jesus, but they don't understand why Jesus is about to lead them into profound danger, even death—his and theirs. Luke takes us inside this historical power struggle, confident that Jesus knew what was happening, without trite answers as to why all of the impending danger must come before Jesus' triumph.

1. Take a pencil and underline the following speakers in today's text. What name or names for Jesus are used by each of these?
    a. The crowds (9:19)
    b. Peter (9:20)
    c. Jesus (9:22 and 26)
    d. God (9:35)

Bonus Activity:

Write a note to yourself or tell a trusted friend if you have had a visionary experience that you didn't talk about until much later.

Tip:

Keep track of the roles that the crowds, Peter, Jesus, and God are given in this historical story. They were real people, and Luke will develop their roles very carefully in the rest of the story.

Tip:

a. The crowds: John the Baptist, Elijah, one of the ancient prophets (9:19)

b. Peter: The Messiah of God (9:20)

c. Jesus: The Son of Man (9:22 and 26)

d. God: my Son, my Chosen (9:35)

Bonus Activity:

If you have some participants with interest in the theater or acting, ask one man and one woman to dress up as Simeon and Anna. Invite them to imagine what they would have said if they came back from the dead to hear Luke's account of the transfiguration. Maybe they heard about it after Jerusalem had been destroyed by the Romans. These are wise Israelites. What do they still hope to see long after Jesus has "accomplished his departure" in Jerusalem? What would still have to happen to bring about the fulfillment of their hopes for "the consolation of Israel" and "the redemption of Jerusalem?"

Bonus Activity:

If someone is interested in "liberation theology" as understood by many people in Latin America, invite them to discuss what kind of "freedom" Jesus brought to his people. Don't argue against this interpretation, but learn from it. This understanding of freedom or liberation is distinct from Martin Luther's interpretation of "The Freedom of the Christian" which is focused on freedom from the need to justify oneself and freedom to be of genuine help to the neighbor.

- How dangerous do you suppose any of those titles would be to Jesus and his followers if a client king of the Romans, such as Herod, or a procurator, such as Pilate, even got wind of a rumor that John the Baptist or Elijah or an ancient prophet had come to life? Who might react most strongly if the word got out that Jesus' followers believed him to be God's Messiah?

- Even the title "Son of Man" that Jesus used was loaded with power. To explore this further, look up Ezekiel 2:1-8 where God sends the son of man with a message of judgment (NRSV translated as "mortal") or see the "son of man" as name for the judge God sends at the end of time (see Daniel 7:13).

2. Martin Luther King's "I Have a Dream" speech includes the specific warning to his followers, "I may not get there with you!" as well as his affirmations that he would also prefer a long life without troubles. He was enacting his understanding of the script of Jesus' journey into the perils of Jerusalem. What sense does it make to you that Martin Luther King sustained his hope in the dream amid real danger? What other big dreams can you think of that were realized only in the face of grave danger?

Lutheran Context

1. Many ancient and modern people who are inspired by Jesus don't like the harsh realities in the Gospel stories, preferring a more "spiritual" vision of Jesus. The ancient "Gnostic" gospels are filled with accounts of Jesus' mysterious sayings and miraculous powers, but they mention almost nothing about his death. The media often hail those versions as more "enlightened" for aiding human "spirituality." Why do you think the cross is offensive to some who want a more "spiritual" Jesus?

2. All four Gospels in the Bible, however, are emphatic about Jesus' marching directly into harm's way in Jerusalem, and they devote large portions of their narratives to Jesus' trial and execution. This is not a story of how humans rose to new spiritual heights but of how God came to the earth to reach us in the flesh. What difference does it make that our salvation or redemption is based on what God "has done," rather than on what we "do"?

3. Martin Luther spoke of "the theology of the cross" as the Christian honesty to call things what they truly are without

glossing over pain and suffering, rejecting a "theology of glory" which denies the reality of evil. God's glory is revealed amid the depths of resistance and violence, not to glorify the violence or suffering, but to "accomplish the exodus," that is, to liberate us from sin, death, and the power of evil.

- An "exodus" is a liberation or a departure from bondage to freedom. Such a rescue often requires great sacrifice from the liberators. Tell a story of a costly rescue operation, perhaps by police or firefighters, maybe by military personnel, or perhaps from your family history. Why were the rescuers willing to take risks and make sacrifices?

4. Moses and Elijah may represent "the law and the prophets" bearing witness to Jesus in the story. Remember that God appeared to each of them in the clouds on a mountain and both had dramatic "departures" at the end of their lives. Notice that the "voice from the cloud" pronounces about Jesus, "This is my Son, my Chosen," while at his baptism, the voice from heaven addressed Jesus directly, "You are my Son, the Beloved" (3:22).

- Have you (or has someone you know) experienced God's presence in some dramatic way? Was it like the stories in the Bible? Why do you suppose God is partially hidden in a cloud or that only God's voice is heard?

Devotional Context

1. The hymn "Son of God, Eternal Savior" (ELW 655) expresses our deep awe for how Jesus enacted God's reign of mercy. Our scripture story reveals that Jesus knew how costly that grace was going to be. God's words from the cloud to Moses, to Elijah, and to Jesus draw us into God's purposes and calling.

- Consider what it means to be God's "Chosen" one. God's voice says, "Listen to him!" What do you expect to hear as Jesus moves forward?

- In *Fiddler on the Roof,* Tevye laments, "God, I know we are the chosen people. But once in a while, can't you choose someone else?" Think about the suffering love of such great saints as Mother Teresa or Dietrich Bonhoeffer. Recall times in your life when you simply had to endure hardship—even deep losses—because of love.

Tip:

Write the words *exodus, rescue, liberation,* and *salvation* on chart paper or a whiteboard. Below those words, write "From what?" and "For what?"

Invite people to explore what we are "saved from" and for what or for whom we are saved. Each of the four words above has its own powerful meaning, but Luke's story does not mince those words. Instead, the story is a strong witness of the "liberation" that Jesus accomplished for us in his "departure." Discipleship involves both drawing near to Jesus and being sent out from him for the blessing of the world.

Tip:

If you have *ELW*s available, provide them to the class for this activity.

Bonus Activity:

Jesus' determination to fulfill his mission grows stronger at every phase of the story. This passion is caught up in the compassion of God, which is the deep mystery in the whole story of why Jesus had to die. To reach this deep level, encourage participants to read aloud the first verse of the hymn "What Wondrous Love Is This" (ELW 666), and then sing all four verses together.

Tip:

Again, let the questions remain open and alive, trusting that the Holy Spirit will reach not only the minds but also the hearts of the participants, sooner or later.

Tip:

As a closing prayer of praise, you could also sing the classic favorite "I Love to Tell the Story" (ELW 661).

2. In our earthly lives, the Bible does not give us spiritual escapes to heavenly bliss, but we are called and sent into the world as God's chosen ones. The promise of heaven on earth awaits the Lord's return. When Peter proposed building three "dwellings" on the mountain, perhaps he was thinking of the shelters the Israelites built on their journey through the wilderness. The Jewish festival of "tabernacles" or "booths" is still celebrated in remembrance of God's deliverance. Maybe Peter wasn't wrong, although Luke reports that Peter made that suggestion, "not knowing what he said" (9:33).

• Tell of a time when you have "come down to earth" from "a mountaintop experience" or spiritual high point in your life. How did you see your daily life differently from that moment on?

Wrap-up

1. If there are any questions to explore further, write them on chart paper or a whiteboard. Ask for volunteers to do further research to share with the group at the next session.

2. What new vision of God's love does this story give to you?

3. What courage does this story give you to be a follower of Jesus?

Pray

How good, Lord, to be here! Your beauty to behold
where Moses and Elijah stand, your messengers of old.
Fulfiller of the past and hope of things to be,
we hail your body glorified and our redemption see.
How good, Lord, to be here! Yet we may not remain;
but since you bid us leave the mount, come with us to the plain.
Amen.
("How Good, Lord, to Be Here!" ELW 315, verses 2, 3, 5)

Extending the Conversation (5 minutes)

Homework

1. Read the next session's Bible text: Luke 15:1–32.

2. For a glimpse of Jesus' determination to accomplish his mission, read Luke 9:51–62. This is the major turning point in the story following the transfiguration when Jesus "turns his face"

and sets his course toward Jerusalem. We already know from his passion predictions (Luke 9:22, 44), that he will be moving into grave danger and death and that those who follow him will share those hazards. Jesus is enacting the prophetic script to "set his face" (Isaiah 50:7; Ezekiel 21:1-2). The confrontation of God's will versus human willfulness lies ahead.

3. Notice in Luke 13:31-35 how Jesus refuses to let some Pharisees (who probably meant well) to protect him from Herod's threats. Although he regularly turns aside to help people in need, Jesus will not be deterred from his mission on his journey to Jerusalem (19:41-44).

Enrichment

1. If you wish to read through the entire book of Luke during this unit, read the following sections this week:

> Day 1: Luke 9:37-62
>
> Day 2: Luke 10:1-24
>
> Day 3: Luke 10:25—11:13
>
> Day 4: Luke 11:14-54
>
> Day 5: Luke 12:1-59
>
> Day 6: Luke 13:1-35
>
> Day 7: Luke 14:1-35

2. When we confess that Jesus was "sacrificed for our sins," we may be thinking about how lambs were sacrificed in the temple and their blood was "poured out." Mark's Gospel (10:45) speaks that way when Jesus tells his disciples that the Son of Man came to give "to give his life a ransom for many." Luke uses very few of the words from the priestly tradition of temple sacrifice, instead describing the conflict with Jesus' adversaries as unavoidable—even necessary—because God intends to rule in mercy and justice. This is the prophetic tradition of God's reign in human history. The prophetic witness understands why it was necessary for Jesus to die in terms of God's conflict against the forces that oppose God. Those include people who are set against God (such as sin), and human principalities protecting their powers (such as the Roman and Jewish rulers), and the forces of evil (such as the demons).

• Write and act out a script of someone who made the "ultimate sacrifice" so that others might live. This might be the story of someone who gave up his or her place in a lifeboat so children would survive , or a soldier who took enemy fire so the others in the squad could find cover.

Tip:
The daily readings for the next two sessions will cover many stories, all of which are rich in content. Encourage people to read each daily assignment slowly, writing comments to themselves about what they are learning about God and Jesus that matters to them.

- Next, think about how Jesus put himself in harm's way, even knowing that he would die, for your liberation from death. The apostle Paul thought deeply about why Jesus had to die in just such terms—to prove God's love for us: "God proves [God's] love for us in that while we were still sinners Christ died for us" (Romans 5:8).

For Further Reading

The Gospel According to Luke by Michael F. Patella in New Collegeville Bible Commentary (Collegeville, MN: Liturgical Press, 2005), pp. 63–67.

"Session 5: Jesus Enacts Scripture" in *Learning Luke: The Apostolic Gospel* with David L. Tiede and friends (www.selectlearning.org).

Provoking the Gospel of Luke: A Storyteller's Commentary by Richard W. Swanson (Cleveland: Pilgrim Press, 2006), pp. 109–112.

Augsburg Commentary on the New Testament: Luke by David L. Tiede (Minneapolis: Augsburg Fortress, 1988), pp. 181–191.

Looking Ahead

1. Read the next session's Bible text: Luke 15:1–32.

2. Read through the Leader Guide for the next session and mark portions you wish to highlight for the group.

3. Make a checklist of any materials you'll need to do the Bonus Activities.

4. Pray for members of your group during the week.

5. Encourage participants to consider what surprises them about God in Jesus' parables.

Luke 15:1–32

Leader Session Guide

Focus Statement

Just when we may be tempted to resent the way Jesus includes people who are not worthy, he invites us to join the rollicking joy in heaven over the return of the lost.

Key Verse

While he was still far off, his father saw him and was filled with compassion; he ran and put his arms around him and kissed him. Luke 15:20

Focus Image

*Return of the Prodigal Son
Rembrandt Harmensz van Rijn
(1606–1669 Dutch)
State Hermitage Museum,
St. Petersburg, Russia
© SuperStock / SuperStock*

Session Preparation

Before You Begin . . .

This session is a gentle time for stories of costly love. The ideas are strong too because Jesus is enacting his reign in ways that are shocking to people who are focused on reasonable righteousness. But the feelings, the compassion, and the yearning for the lost are not merely ideas. Don't rush. Take time to center yourself. Remember a time when you loved someone who didn't deserve it, beyond all sense and reason. Or maybe you have experienced such love yourself when you knew you weren't worthy of receiving it. The extravagance of God's love surpasses the calculations of righteous worth. Believe it!

Session Instructions

1. Read this Session Guide completely and highlight or underline any portions you wish to emphasize with the group. Note any Bonus Activities you wish to do.

2. If you plan to do any special activities, check to see what materials you'll need, if any.

3. Have extra Bibles on hand in case a member of the group forgets to bring one.

Session Overview

Taken out of context, the story of the **prodigal** son has often been used as a morality lesson about not wasting the family's resources and reputation. That message is present in the story, but taken together, the stories of the lost sheep, the lost coin, and the lost son draw us into the world of God's love for the lost. Maybe this is more aptly called the story of the waiting father. From the point of view of "What will the neighbors think?" this is the story of the prodigality of the father's love. And in the still larger context of Luke 14 and the criticism of the Pharisees in Luke 15:1–2, this is another revelation of Jesus' refusal to be distracted while enacting God's compassion for those who need it most.

LITERARY CONTEXT

The New Testament stories about Jesus eating with tax collectors and sinners are alive to the question "Who is invited into God's kingdom?" Who are God's chosen ones, the elect? We understand this humanly from our own experience of the inclusion and

? Prodigal:

This story has come to define the meaning of the word prodigal, even in the dictionaries. It is an old English word used to describe someone who is "given to extravagant expenditure; recklessly wasteful of one's property or means" (see the Oxford English Dictionary), and in societies based on property, that waste may be the great offense. Preoccupation with the lurid details of the younger son's behavior has characterized much of the moralistic history of interpretation. First century hearers might have been most scandalized by the image of this Jewish boy eating among pigs or the elder son's assertion that the younger had wasted the property on prostitutes (Luke 15:30).

? Pharisees:

As emphasized by the comments in this session, the Pharisees were members of a popular movement seeking observance of the practices of God's law in local synagogues and in the homes of the people. They were not the powerful rulers in the temple, and they apparently tried to protect Jesus from the tyrants (Luke 13:31; 19:39).

exclusion of who gets invited to a wedding or a child's birthday party. But what if it is God's party, and the Messiah himself keeps bringing in people who don't keep the law?

The Learner Session Guide intends to let people feel the force of Jesus' stories, to step into the characters and let God's magnificent mercy surprise them. Listen carefully for a moment when a participant catches on to point that God's love is excessive, even unreasonable. If the angels of God rejoice extravagantly when one sinner repents (Luke 15:10, see also 15:7), what is the delight they are feeling? How do we get in on it?

HISTORICAL CONTEXT

Make sure that the historical context doesn't allow the participants to get self-righteous in their criticism of the first century **Pharisees.** The point, rather, is that we are like them. To sense the enduring force of Jesus' words, a distinguished Presbyterian scholar translates Luke 15:2 saying, "the Presbyterians and the scribes were grumbling." We could as well say, "The Lutherans and the scholars were grumbling" because Jesus' teaching continues to be shocking to all self-respecting religious people.

Historical studies of the first century have opened new understanding of how close Jesus and his followers were to the scribes and teachers of the Pharisaic movement. The apostle Paul identified himself as "a Hebrew born of Hebrews; as to the law, a Pharisee" (Philippians 3:5), and Jesus was enacting God's reign, for which the Pharisees had already labored for generations in order to prepare the people.

In Jesus' time, both the Pharisees and the Messianists (followers of Jesus the Messiah) were members of popular movements, poring over the scriptures and expecting the fulfillment of God's promises. But what faithfulness was needed? A strict observance of God's law in preparation for the Messiah or a joyful trust in Jesus as God's ruler come to earth?

Without getting entangled in the complicated history of the disputes and struggles between those two movements, make sure the participants understand: a) everyone in these stories is Jewish; b) Jesus and the Pharisees continue to mix it up throughout the story; and c) Jesus' enactment of God's love is still shocking to religious people, even today.

This is also not the time for elaborate discussions of how Jesus' reign of compassion was a threat to the **Roman Order,** but it is helpful to remember that Jesus did not teach in a vacuum, apart from the real world. Even the Apostles' Creed highlights that Jesus was "crucified under Pontius Pilate," and Luke has surrounded these stories with gathering storm clouds.

The goal of reviewing the historical context is to help participants be aware of the social and political forces that still surround their Christian lives. Jesus did not displace the government of his time, nor did he run for office. He did, however, disclose that God is at work in the world, including the social and political realm. Rather than lecturing about first-century politics, the best way to engage this reality is in listening for stories of how tyrants continue to be distressed by Christian love and hope. A Christian leader who had experienced persecution from a hostile dictator once asked a group, "If you were on trial for being a follower of Jesus, would there be evidence to convict you?" Yet Jesus' followers still experience rejection. Why?

Lutheran Context

Martin Luther was deeply distressed because even when he confessed his sins, observing all the strict practices of penance, he could not cleanse himself. Evil thoughts and desires still crept in. The problem was not a lack of sincere effort. With the apostle Paul, Luther confessed, "I find it to be a law that when I want to do what is good, evil lies close at hand. . . . Wretched man that I am! Who will rescue me from this body of death?" And with Paul he rejoiced, "Thanks be to God through Jesus Christ our Lord!" (Romans 7:14–25)

The hope in the story lies not in the sincerity of the younger son who returns but in the compassion of the father who welcomes him. Loving parents who break the rules in order to rescue their child are enacting God's reign of mercy. These human stories are all around us. First, let people tell about someone else: the lurid tales in the tabloids of the fall of the famous; the shame of a grandfather who bailed out his grandson from detox one more time; the mother who accompanied her daughter through an unplanned pregnancy or even nursed her to health after an abortion; the family that always believed homosexuality to be a sin who then welcomed their partnered child at the reunion. This is not a time for judgment. The elder brothers and the Pharisees may still speak, but where is God's reign of compassion

? Roman Order:

The *Roman Order* is a term for the whole system of laws, administration, and civil religion of the Roman Empire. The official "piety" of Rome was vested in temples and sacrifices that honored the emperor. As long as the Jews offered prayers and sacrifices on behalf of the emperor and the realm, they were tolerated within the "Roman Order" because of the great age of their tradition.

at work? If it were easy, Christ would not have had to have died to rescue us.

DEVOTIONAL CONTEXT

The challenge is to find ways to recognize this tension that is already at work in participants' lives. The exercises in the Learner Session Guide may be helpful. But it will only take one story from a participant about how he or she abandoned self-righteousness because they loved a lost child. ("God help us! What else could we do?")

These stories of reconciliation are painful, but they disclose God's power and presence. If someone ventures to tell about the price they paid to reach out to a child or a brother or sister who had gone over the edge, slow down. Listen carefully. Know that others in the room are disturbed, and let the Spirit of Christ Jesus move among you.

Self-righteousness is nurtured in denial and compounded by the judgment of others. Even many people who are not Christian have been blessed by Jesus' profound trust in the power of God's surpassing love, holding them when their own power had failed. The famous "Serenity Prayer" was adopted by Alcoholics Anonymous from an earlier version by Christian theologian and pastor Reinhold Niebuhr.

> God, grant me the serenity
> To accept the things I cannot change;
> Courage to change the things I can;
> And wisdom to know the difference.

Facilitator's Prayer

O God, where is there another like you? You forgive sin and forgive the iniquity of the lowest of your people. You do not stay angry forever, for you are merciful and you pardon our transgressions and cast all our sins into the deep sea. Do continue to be merciful, so that we may walk in the light of your Word and escape every trap of Satan and of the world, through Jesus Christ, your Son, our Redeemer. Amen.
(From Luther's Prayers, ed. Herbert F. Brokering (Minneapolis: Augsburg Fortress, 1994).)

Gather (10–15 minutes)

Check–in

Invite learners to share completed homework or any new thoughts or insights about the previous session. Be ready to give a brief recap of that session if necessary.

Pray

Heavenly Father, we thank you that you are more ready to welcome our return than we are to come to you. We admit that our pride tempts us to be self-righteous, even resentful, when your compassion extends to people we regard as unworthy. But when we are the ones whom you welcome while we are still far off, or when someone we love returns home, we join the angels in heaven in praising your amazing grace. Open now our hearts and minds to learn the ways of your compassion and to rejoice in Jesus' love. Amen.

Focus Activity

Take a quiet moment to recall a time in your own life when someone loved you, even though you did not deserve it. Maybe it was a teacher or a parent or grandparent or a friend who stood by you when others were disapproving. If you could thank that person today, what would you say? How did such love empower you to care for someone else?

Open Scripture (10–15 minutes)

One option is to invite your best storyteller to recite this chapter with feeling.

A second option is to hear the passage from several voices speaking as narrator and various characters. Ask for volunteers to speak when the characters speak (the woman who lost her coin; the father, prodigal, and older brother; the Pharisees and teachers of the law).

A third option is to divide up the reading into several sections and ask several volunteers to read.

Tip:
Take particular care to welcome people warmly to this session. Many will have come from frantic lives. Help them now dwell in the joy and wonder of God's mercy.

Tip:
Be calm, rest easy, and know (in the words of the old English prayer), "Bidden or unbidden, God is here!"

Tip:
Invite participants to discuss in pairs, or ask for volunteers to share stories with the whole group.

Tip:
This is a long reading. Make sure that anyone who reads has had time to prepare and to consider how these words from Jesus have transformed countless lives of people who could hardly believe that the story they heard was truly God's story.

Tip:

Gather some initial responses to the questions on chart paper. Keep them in view as the conversation continues.

Tip:

If you search on the Internet for "Prodigal Son," you will find a remarkable collection of art as well as rich resources from the religions of the world.

Bonus Activity:

Encourage a participant to review Robert M. Brusic's book, *And Grace Will Lead Me Home* (Lutheran University Press, 2007). This is a study of the extensive collection that Jerry A. Evenrud donated to Luther Seminary in St. Paul, Minnesota. For an inventory of the full collection, visit this site: www. luthersem.edu/prodigal

Tip:

To appreciate the power of these stories, ask someone to give the elder son's speech in Luke 15:29–30 as a serious and highly responsible testimony. Yes, it is an angry speech, but it is also sensible for those who are confident of their morality.

Read Luke 15:1–32.

- What caught your attention when you heard these three stories read together?
- Are any of the characters in the stories unreasonable or even unfair?
- Did you learn anything surprising about God in these familiar stories? If so, what?

Join the Conversation (25–55 minutes)

Literary Context

1. All three of the stories in Luke 15 are popular and beloved, even by people who have never read Luke's Gospel. Taken together, all three stories in Luke 15 explore what Jesus revealed in Luke 14 about the hospitality of God's kingdom, rejecting standard protocols for banqueting with the elect and the elite. Luke also introduces these stories as Jesus' direct response to the criticism of the Pharisees and the scribes in 15:2—"This fellow welcomes sinners and eats with them."

- What common theme or themes do you see connecting these stories in Luke 15?
- Think about the characters in each of the stories. What motivates them to do what they do? Which character surprised you the most? Why? With which character do you most identify? Why?

2. Every grade school child knows how it feels to be included or excluded from a birthday party, and adults are also quick to look for their own names on guest lists. Those who are "chosen" are the "elect," and the others often feel unworthy.

- Whom does Jesus invite to the table in the story in Luke 14:7–14? What parallel do you see between that story and the stories in Luke 15?
- Make a guest list for your church's next anniversary. What would the church be like—what would our lives be like—if we followed Jesus' counsel to his host in Luke 14:12–14?

3. Attempts to interpret Jesus' parables as morality stories, like Aesop's fables, stumble over obvious realities. The shepherd was not prudent in leaving 99 sheep in the wilderness. The woman was obsessed with finding a small coin to the point that her party for her neighbors probably cost more than the coin was worth.

- What about the younger son (the prodigal)? What seems obvious about what he deserves?

- And what about the older son, the prodigal's brother? Is his reaction expected or not? Why?

- Look again at the older son's speech in 15:29–30. Put the elder son's words in the context of the grumbling from the Pharisees and the scribes about Jesus: "This fellow welcomes sinners and eats with them" (Luke 15:2). What similarities do you see?

Historical Context

1. Who were the Pharisees? The Pharisees were not bad people. In modern times, non-Jewish Christians often use the word "Pharisee" as an insult to or about people they regard as rigid and self-righteous. It is important to remember that according to Luke, Jesus dined in the house of a Pharisee at least twice (Luke 7:36–50; 11:37–41), and some of the believers in Acts are identified as belonging "to the sect of the Pharisees" (Acts 15:5). Yes, these stories are marked with tension over whether the Pharisees could accept Jesus' remarkable acceptance of outsiders, but Luke presents Jesus as a teacher among the Pharisees and reminds us that some of the Pharisees belonged to the "believers." These Pharisees were not adversaries, but followers of Jesus.

- Look at the piece of art above entitled *Christ and the Pharisees*. Most art that depicts Jesus and the Pharisees shows the biblical scenes when they are in conflict. What strikes you about this scene? Do you think of Jesus as being a teacher "among" the Pharisees? How (if at all) does that affect the way you think of the relationship between Jesus and the Pharisees?

2. "The Pharisees and the scribes" worked together to renew Israel's faithfulness to God. The scriptures were copied by the scribes to be circulated in the synagogues. Those of us who are writing these materials for the Book of Faith initiative are modern scribes. The Pharisees were members of a reform movement, calling Israel to obedience to God's law. Some of them criticized the way that certain high priests collaborated with the Greek or Roman occupation forces to keep their positions or abused their office for personal gain. Some Pharisees were crucified by the tyrants. The Pharisees also taught the people how to keep their homes and their synagogues purified according to God's law.

- Have you ever considered the positive contribution that the Pharisees and scribes made to Jewish life and faith? Why or why not?

Christ and the Pharisees
by Edward Armitage
(1817–1896 British)
© SuperStock / SuperStock

 Bonus Activity:

If someone is interested in learning more about the Pharisees, a good place to start is the brief article "Pharisees" by Anthony J. Saldarini in *Harper's Biblical Dictionary* (San Francisco: HarperOne 1985), pp. 782–83.

- It is easy to criticize the Pharisees, but what if they are like your neighbors or like you? They were striving to do the right thing, but they were tempted to be more judgmental than compassionate! Why is it easy to judge others but more difficult to walk in another's shoes?

3. What about modern Christian Pharisees? There is an old joke about a person who objected to serving wine at communion. The pastor observed, "Yes, but Jesus drank wine." "Oh, I know that," said the objector, "but that's the one thing I don't like about Jesus!" Give the Pharisees a break. Consider these stories from their point of view, or from the elder brother's point of view. Write a paragraph that expresses their reasonable objection. What is "the one thing you don't like about Jesus" if you are one of the "ninety-nine righteous persons who need no repentance" (Luke 15:7)?

4. Consider Jesus from the point of view of the Roman occupation forces. The Roman world was run by "Law and Order!"; generally, it was well run, but there was also a dark side to Roman systems of discipline and control. This harsher view will be evident in Session 7 on Jesus' trial and execution. Imagine a scene in Herod's court or in Pilate's palace. In Luke 9:9, Herod was already musing, "John I beheaded; but who is this about whom I hear such things?" And Jesus already mentioned Pilate as the tyrant who mixed the blood of the Galileans with their sacrifices (Luke 13:1). The Pharisees are the ones who warned Jesus, "Herod wants to kill you" (13:31).

- Imagine that you are Herod or Pilate and you have heard rumors, maybe inaccurate stories, about a prophet-teacher who is traveling the countryside, announcing God's reign of compassion, love for the unworthy, and acceptance of outsiders. Why would you want that prophet-teacher out of the way?

Lutheran Context

1. The Lutheran confession of the gospel is an invitation to saving trust in God's love. "While we were still sinners Christ died for us," declared Paul (Romans 5:8). "For by grace you have been saved through faith, and this is not your own doing; it is the gift of God" (Ephesians 2:8). Where do you see this "gospel" message played out in the story of the prodigal?

Tip:

Approach this question with some sensitivity. It is easy for each of us to determine what the "rules" are for others and not see where we may need direction ourselves. It is also easy to view the life of faith as following certain rules. Jesus did things that did not follow the religious rules of his own tradition. The older brother follows the rules and just wants what he deserves. He feels his younger brother went outside the rules. Why should that rule-breaking be celebrated?

Tip:

"Justification by faith" means trusting that God makes us righteous. The word *righteous* is commonly used to speak of people who are morally upright. Following Paul, Luther testified that when we are clothed in our human righteousness, we are only wearing "rags." The robe the Father puts on us is the righteousness of heaven.

2. The elder son was religiously righteous. He probably would have been more concerned with protecting the ninety-nine sheep who had not strayed and less impressed by the extravagant preoccupation by the shepherd or the woman about the one that was lost.

- Do you think the elder brother believed his younger brother's confession, "Father, I have sinned against heaven and before you. I am no longer worthy to be called your son," or do you think he suspected that the younger brother was still manipulating the situation? Why or why not?

- If it is true that "while we were still sinners Christ died for us," does it matter whether the elder son has read his brother correctly or if the younger son's return/repentance was truly genuine? Why or why not? From a "gospel perspective," what does matter?

3. Imagine the parable of the prodigal in a modern setting. For example, consider a loving parent who lavishes time and resources on a child who is in trouble with himself/herself, the law, and the world. How many times will the "lost one" go to rehab? And what is a sober, responsible sibling going to think? Even when a parent's searching and abundant love is not able to rescue the lost, this "amazing grace" is a human enactment of God's compassion. Have you experienced or seen examples of such "grace-filled" love and compassion?

Devotional Context

1. These stories reveal the deep mystery of the joy of heaven in recovering the lost. The compassion of the father is more than the wayward son can expect, and his extravagant love can hardly be grasped or tolerated by the righteous son. Freed from self-righteousness, the faithful relinquish their right to envy God's reception of the wayward. "How blessed are those who know their need of God." Only forgiven sinners stand at the foot of the cross.

- When have you acted like the younger brother, the older brother, or the father?

- Who are the lost, those who want or need to be welcomed home?

Tip:

Ultimately, what matters is that the Father's compassion overflows for an unworthy child, rushing down the road to him and not even waiting for him to complete his apology. When Lutherans get this right—following Jesus, Paul, and the Gospels—they abandon their efforts to judge the repentance of others or even of themselves, trusting merely in God's astonishing love, enacted in Christ Jesus.

Bonus Activity:

This would be an excellent session for a visit to a Lutheran Social Service program or a visit from one of their staff members. Pay particular attention to people who do this work. Notice how freely they care for people who are often regarded by others as useless. Lutheran social ministries are known for reaching out to people who are at risk, without consideration of whether those who need help are "worthy," Lutheran, or even Christian. Invite a staff member from Lutheran Social Service or some other agency to meet with your group. Why must they always treat their clients with great respect? Ask them to tell about a time when they experienced the "joy of the angels" in dealing with a client who is unlikely to express gratitude or repay the kindness. How can those who support this work sense God at work in their gifts?

Bonus Activity:

Extend an invitation to a participant or guest who has experienced the transforming power of God's love to tell his or her story. Be careful to respect the anonymity of people in recovery programs, and be aware that learners in your class may be reluctant to share their personal stories. Don't intrude, but welcome any stories that people are comfortable sharing about how God's amazing grace has worked in their lives and families.

2. Take a walk into the chancel of your church. Who is welcome at the Lord's table (Holy Communion) in your congregation? Who decides who is welcome, and do all agree with these procedures or policies? What, if anything, might you change? Why? Do you think it pleases God when sinners join Jesus' meal? Do you think it is responsible to insist on some moral standards, some observance of God's law, or some evidence of true repentance for admission to the table?

3. Look at the Focus Image once again. After what you have read and discussed, what other titles might you give to this painting? Why?

4. What prayer or prayers do these stories prompt for you?

Wrap-up

1. If there are any questions to explore further, write them on chart paper or a whiteboard. Ask for volunteers to do further research to share with the group at the next session.

2. Ask people to think about the following questions:

- Why are you glad that God chose to love you before you made yourself righteous?
- Do you think that God's strategy of loving sinners can save the world?

Pray

God of compassion, you welcome the wayward, and you embrace all with your mercy. By our baptism clothe us with garments of your grace, and feed us at the table of your love, through Jesus Christ, our Savior and Lord, who lives and reigns with you and the Holy Spirit, one God, now and forever. Amen.
(Prayer for Fourth Sunday in Lent, Year C, ELW, p. 28)

 Tip:
For your closing prayer, you might also consider singing together on all verses of "Amazing Grace, How Sweet the Sound" (ELW 779). You may wish to have a musician who can lead or accompany the singing.

Extending the Conversation (5 minutes)

Homework

1. Read the next session's Bible text: Luke 23:26–49.

2. The Gospel story reveals not only the extravagance of God's love but also its cost. As you read the chapters in Luke prior to the next meeting of the Book of Faith group, make a list of the places where Jesus knows 1) what this mission of love will cost him and 2) how costly it will be for Jesus' followers in the mission ahead.

3. Pay a visit to one of the older saints in your congregation or a couple who have been married for decades. Ask them to tell you about when their love was tested in sorrow or brokenness. What price did they or someone pay because "that's what you do when you love someone?" How were they assured of God's love for them through the dark time?

Enrichment

1. If you wish to read through the entire book of Luke during this unit, read the following sections this week:

   Day 1: Luke 16:1–31

   Day 2: Luke 17:1–37

   Day 3: Luke 18:1–30

   Day 4: Luke 18:31–19:10

   Day 5: Luke 19:11–47

   Day 6: Luke 20:1–26

   Day 7: Luke 20:27–47

2. In this session, Jesus' parables are revelations of God's gracious reign, not mere lessons in behavior. Many Bible dictionaries have good, brief introductions to the interpretation of Jesus' parables as the "riddles" or "revelations" of God's reign. Some interpreters have argued that our understanding of Jesus' parables has been distorted by moralizing their messages, thereby missing the mystery of God that they disclose.

• Read one or more of the brief Bible dictionary articles on "parables" and alert the group to the ways that Jesus surprised his listeners in each of these parables.

 Tip:
Encourage the participants to consider the two "homework" assignments, the first on taking some notes on the weekly readings and the second on listening to the saints.

- When Jesus tells of the love of the father, he is echoing the witness of Israel's prophets to God's compassion, even God's pathos, or suffering, when the people have lost their way. Read Ezekiel 34, for example, to hear God's anguish as well as God's commitment to bring the people—not just an individual—to safety: "I myself will search for my sheep, and will seek them out."

For Further Reading

The Gospel According to Luke by Michael F. Patella in New Collegeville Bible Commentary Series (Collegeville, MN: Liturgical Press, 2005), pp. 102–107.

"Session 7: Parables and Revelation" in *Learning Luke: The Apostolic Gospel* with David L. Tiede and friends (*www. selectlearning.org*).

Provoking the Gospel of Luke: A Storyteller's Commentary by Richard W. Swanson (Cleveland: Pilgrim Press, 2006), pp. 128–134, 193–198.

Augsburg Commentary on the New Testament: Luke by David L. Tiede (Minneapolis: Augsburg Fortress, 1988), pp. 272–281.

Looking Ahead

1. Read the next session's Bible text: Luke 23:26–49.

2. Read through the Leader Guide for the next session and mark portions you wish to highlight for the group.

3. Make a checklist of any materials you'll need to do the Bonus Activities.

4. Pray for members of your group during the week.

5. Prepare yourself to move from the sweetness of Jesus' parables to the agony of his death.

Luke 23:26–49

Ah, Holy Jesus, How Hast Thou Offended?

Leader Session Guide

Focus Statement

The execution of Jesus tested all of God's promises of justice and mercy. Standing at the foot of the cross, we are both tormented and deeply inspired by what we see and hear.

Key Verse

When the centurion saw what had taken place, he praised God and said, "Certainly this man was innocent."
Luke 23:47

Focus Image

Pardoning of the Penitent Thief
James Tissot (1836–1902/French)
© SuperStock / SuperStock

Session Preparation

Before You Begin . . .

We rejoiced at Jesus' birth when God came to earth to be among us. Now, we will stand on the most evil ground in human history—which is also the holiest ground—because it is here that God met human beings at their worst, not to destroy but to save them. Take time to contemplate the meaning of the cross for you. How is your life different because of this event?

Session Instructions

1. Read this Session Guide completely and highlight or underline any portions you wish to emphasize with the group. Note any Bonus Activities you wish to do.

2. If you plan to do any special activities, check to see what materials you'll need, if any.

3. Have extra Bibles on hand in case a member of the group forgets to bring one.

4. Bring several crosses or crucifixes (with the figure of Jesus still on the cross).

Session Overview

This session is the culmination of Jesus' journey to Jerusalem, which we have been following since his presentation in the temple in Jerusalem when he was eight days old. The evangelist (Luke), often quoting Jesus, has alerted us that suffering and death lie ahead. Jesus walks into a hostile reception in Jerusalem. The leaders in the temple regard him as a threat, and the Romans have come up from Caesarea to quell any insurrection provoked by the Jewish Passover. This is a story of God's profound redemption in the midst of brutal politics. The goal of the session is to help participants understand that they are not merely watching an ancient drama, but that their own salvation and the hope of the world are being enacted by Jesus in his determined mission, faithful unto death.

LITERARY CONTEXT

This is a session for appreciating Luke's literary art, not merely for its elegance but also for how this telling of "the events that have been fulfilled among us" (Luke 1:1) are evident to the eyes of faith but hidden from many of the people in the drama.

Following the prophetic witness that God's adversaries can't see or hear what God is truly doing with their physical hearing or sight (see Isaiah 6:9–10 and Luke 8:10), Luke emphasizes that the people who sought to protect Jesus, then failed, were now "beating their breasts" at his impending death (Luke 23:27), and then again when they actually "saw what had taken place" (Luke 23:48). We "stand at a distance" with Jesus' acquaintances, including the women who had followed him from Galilee, "watching these things" (Luke 23:49). The evangelist invites us to see God at work, accomplishing our salvation in the midst of these terrors.

Watch for how the **sarcasm** of Jesus' adversaries **ironically** testifies to the truth of who Jesus is and what God is doing. Each of the titles for Jesus has been explored in previous sessions: Messiah of God, his Chosen One, and King of the Jews. Now these titles are thrown at Jesus in derision, but by God's good plan, they reveal who he is.

Perhaps participants could be asked to recall a time when someone intended to be sarcastic but still spoke the truth without even knowing it. Comedians often make jokes that strike close to the truth, and the **tragic dramas** understand this well, whether speaking of King Lear or Oedipus.

Israel's Scriptures were prepared for attacks on God's son and "righteous one." Wisdom of Solomon, written about two centuries before Jesus, testified that God's authorization of the "righteous" or "innocent" one will confront those who ridicule God's purposes. Wisdom of Solomon 2:17-22 says, "'. . . let us test what will happen at the end of his life; for if the righteous man is God's [child], he will help him,'" then continues, "Thus they reasoned, but they were led astray, for their wickedness blinded them, and they did not know the secret purposes of God . . ."

The Learner Session Guide proposes that the participants first speak the sarcastic charges, then restate them as testimonies of faith. The evangelist knows from scripture and Jesus that God is on the side of the truth of these testimonies.

? Sarcasm:

This is more than grim or mean humor. It is intended to ridicule the truths that others hold dear. Stand-up comics regularly practice sarcasm in order to expose what they regard as pompous or manipulative claims. The prophet Elijah also practiced sarcasm in mocking the priests of Baal (1 Kings 18:20–40).

? Irony:

This is the truth side of sarcasm because that which is being ridiculed is true, even if the speaker does not know it to be true. In placing the charge over Jesus' head at his crucifixion, the Roman executioners proclaimed him "King of the Jews," adding a testimony to Jesus as the Messiah of Israel.

? Tragic Dramas:

Scholars debate whether Luke's story of Jesus is tragic because it has many of the characteristics and even the literary forms of the Greek and Roman tragic histories and dramas. It should be noted, however, that unlike tragic figures in those histories or dramas, Jesus is never blind to what he has done or what will happen to him. He is not a tragic hero but an obedient Son of his Heavenly Father.

HISTORICAL CONTEXT

In addition to exploring the map of Jerusalem in Jesus' Time on p. 84, review the map of Palestine in Jesus' Time on p. 8 of the Learner Session Guide. Judea was one of several provinces ruled by Rome but with some amount of local governance as well. You could point out that Pilate usually resided in Caesarea and that Herod Antipas ruled Galilee and Perea from his palace in Tiberias.

The point is that Jesus was not crucified on a church altar between two candles, but between two criminals in the dust and wind of a Roman execution. The exercises suggested in the Learner Session Guide seek to highlight the reality of this historical context, which was a volatile political setting. Jesus' ministry was causing waves among some of the religious leaders of his own Jewish people. Since those leaders could not lawfully execute Jesus, they needed the help of the Roman government, whose local provincial leader was Pontius Pilate.

At the same time, Herod Antipas, son of Herod the Great, wanted to be recognized as king of the Jews. He played power games back and forth between his own people and the Romans. A teacher and miracle worker like Jesus, who had strong backing by many people, would have attracted his attention. But neither Herod nor Pilate found Jesus guilty of any crime, including inciting an uprising. Even so, those who feared Jesus most convinced the powers that be to execute Jesus.

LUTHERAN CONTEXT

It is important to remember that the "theology of the cross" is not a glorification of suffering but the glorification of God who transforms Jesus' suffering into salvation. The Learner Session Guide emphasizes the reality of the suffering, just as Christians who experience suffering never need to deny its force. In Luke's Gospel, Jesus prayed on the Mount of Olives that the cup of suffering might be removed from him (Luke 22:44). Jesus' obedience to God was his trust that God would bring a greater salvation from his death.

Spend some time with Luther's explanation to the second article of the Apostles' Creed. Although Luther does not specifically mention the cross, it is clear that Jesus' work of redemption was accomplished through the cross, where his blood and innocent suffering and death freed us from sin, death, and the power of the devil.

This might be a good occasion to invite a hospice nurse or physician to speak with the group. How has that person's experience allowed him or her to observe that the people who are suffering and dying are sustained by their faith in God?

DEVOTIONAL CONTEXT

It is only through prayer, praise, and thanksgiving that mere mortals can begin to understand the mysteries of Jesus' suffering, relying on Pascal's wisdom that "the heart has reasons [that] reason knows not of!" Even in the confusion, terror, and sorrow of Jesus' gruesome death, Christian believers begin to sense the joy and hope of the "exodus" that Jesus is fulfilling for us and the world in Jerusalem. Jesus himself spoke of this "saving journey" when he said: "I have a baptism with which to be baptized" (Luke 12:50).

This story is a matter of death and life, and it will be well to maintain a deep reverence. The traditional "words" of Jesus from the cross provide the opportunity for participants to explore the meaning of Jesus' mission and to seek their own part in that ongoing mission.

Facilitator's Prayer

Lord Jesus, you went on your way into suffering and a cruel death, trusting that your Heavenly Father's loving purpose would thus be accomplished. In your prayer on the Mount of Olives, you agonized, asking if there was not another way. Be with me now, Lord Jesus. Some of our participants are enduring their own suffering, not knowing why it is happening or how it will end. Help me to point them to you, that they may know you have already shared their human agonies and that God has brought redemption to them and the whole world through your innocent suffering and death. Amen.

Gather (10–15 minutes)

Check–in

Invite learners to share completed homework or any new thoughts or insights about the previous session. Be ready to give a brief recap of that session if necessary.

Tip:
This would be a good time to point out the variety of crosses and crucifixes you have brought to the session. Let people touch, compare, and explore their differences.

Pray

Almighty God, look with loving mercy on your family, for whom our Lord Jesus Christ was willing to be betrayed, to be given over to the hands of sinners, and to suffer death on the cross; who now lives and reigns with you and the Holy Spirit, one God, forever and ever. Amen. (Collect for Good Friday, ELW, p. 31)

Focus Activity

Remember a time when you experienced how unfair life can be. Maybe it was something that was done to you. Maybe you watched as others were mean or even brutal to a childhood friend or a vulnerable person. Maybe it was a wartime experience. Maybe you participated in ways you now regret. Then remember Jesus' own innocent suffering. Write a confidential prayer, calling God to forgive and care for all who suffer.

Tip:
Be especially reverent, perhaps darkening your meeting space, like on Good Friday.

Open Scripture (10–15 minutes)

Once again, this is a fairly long reading. Its flow may commend using one reader who can read slowly and with expression. As an alternative, you could use a narrator and assign the voices to read the parts of Jesus, Soldier(s), Criminal 1, Criminal 2, and Centurion.

Tip:
Again, move reverently, especially if you or someone in the group invites the others into the holy ground of their lives where they are still aware of sadness or failing others.

Read Luke 23:26–49.

- What do you find most troubling about this story of Jesus' execution?
- What would you have thought if you walked in on this crucifixion from somewhere else without knowing what was happening?
- What words or actions by the people described in this passage surprise you the most?

Tip:
Give volunteer readers a few moments to identify their parts, if you are doing the reading in dramatic form.

Join the Conversation (25–55 minutes)

Literary Context

1. Luke carefully identifies the differing roles of all who are present at Jesus' execution. Look at the Focus Image for this session. What characters can you identify based on Luke's depiction of the crucifixion?

Tip:

Restating the mocking words as confessions of faith might go something like this: "He saved others; save us, Jesus, because you truly are God's Messiah and chosen one!" "Since you are the King of the Jews; save us too, Jesus, because your love extends to all the people of the earth." And "You truly are the Messiah! Because you did not save yourself, you will save us."

Bonus Activity:

Invite learners to imagine what the key characters in this crucifixion drama were like before their lives were thrown together at the cross. Develop a brief "profile" of the criminals, the centurion, Simon of Cyrene, or one of the mourning women. Each profile would be simple, providing age, hometown, interests, etc., or a bit longer, explaining how the person/the people happen to be present at this moment in history. Those who like to draw could add a picture.

CITY OF JERUSALEM IN JESUS' TIME

City of Jerusalem in Jesus' Time
Lutheran Study Bible, p. 2110

Tip:

Some people may be distressed by the highly political character of Jesus' crucifixion, but the wonder is how God did something so spiritually transformative in the midst of the human struggles for authority in Jesus' time.

- What "attitude" is displayed toward Jesus by the Roman soldiers, Jewish leaders, and the first criminal?
- Recite aloud the derisive comments of the leaders (verse 35), the soldiers (verses 36–37), and the first criminal (verse 39), first in their evil tone of voice.

2. Notice the sign that is put above Jesus' head on the cross: "This is the King of the Jews" (23:38). The political point of the execution was to warn against any who would dare to claim non-Roman authority to rule. But we know that their sarcastic threats actually tell the truth. How could the sarcastic and mocking statements in verses 35–39 be turned into confessions of faith?

3. The Roman centurion's words stand in contrast to the mocking earlier in the scene. The centurion "saw what had taken place" with the eyes of faith. Recite verse 47 with particular care for how he declares Jesus "innocent." This word could also be translated as "righteous." Whatever the centurion meant to say, (see also Mark 15:39, "God's Son"), the early Christians understood his declaration as identifying Jesus as God's promised "Righteous One" (Acts 3:14; 7:52; 22:14).

- What significance do you see in the words of the centurion, who was supposed to swear allegiance to the emperor?
- What about those who "returned home, beating their breasts" (23:48)? You might be helped to know that the word in Greek for "returned home" is literally "they turned" or even "they repented." What do you suppose they were saying to themselves about what they had just seen and heard as they turned away to go home?

Historical Context

1. Every Sunday when we recite the Apostles' Creed in worship, we remember that Jesus Christ was "crucified under Pontius Pilate." Jesus was his given name, and Christ means Messiah or "anointed one." In Israel, the kings were not crowned, but like King David, Jesus was anointed on divine authority with the Holy Spirit and with power (see 1 Samuel 16; Psalm 2; Acts 10:38).

Read Luke 23:1–12. Keep in mind that both the Roman procurator Pontius Pilate and Herod Antipas were in Jerusalem only because of the Passover.

- Look at the map (p. 51) and note key locations mentioned in the trials and crucifixion of Jesus. Pilate most likely headquartered at the Fortress Antonia. Jesus was arrested in the Garden of Gethsemane, taken to the High Priest's house, and then shuttled back and forth between Pilate and Herod Antipas before going to the cross on Golgotha.

- What were the charges against Jesus that might have provoked the Roman procurator, Pontius Pilate? What question does Pilate ask Jesus? How does Jesus answer? What does Pilate conclude from this answer?

- The Roman Senate named Herod the Great "The King of the Jews" (see Matthew 2:1), and Caesar Augustus (see Luke 2) gave him authority to rule in Judea and Galilee. His sons were not given this title, but Herod Antipas, who appears in Luke's story, yearned to be named "King of the Jews," provoking animosity with Pilate, the Roman procurator (see Luke 23:12). Based on that, why do you think this question was important to Pilate?

2. Pilate sends Jesus to Herod Antipas. Why? How does Herod treat Jesus? Why do you think Herod and Pilate "became friends with each other" on that particular day? How genuine and/or cynical do you think the "friendship" was that Herod and Pilate formed in Jesus' trial?

3. Why it is still important to non–Jewish Christians that Jesus was truly "King of the Jews"?

4. If Pilate does not find Jesus guilty of any crime, why does he eventually sentence Jesus to death by crucifixion? Who had the most to gain by getting Jesus out of the way?

5. The Romans used crucifixion to execute the most despicable criminals and "enemies of the Roman Order." No conquered nation, including Judea, could conduct a crucifixion without Roman authority. It was a public display of their power, intended to shame the victims and terrify all who were present. Even when worn as an ornament or jewelry, the cross continues to remind us of a brutal and humiliating death.

- All four Gospels in the New Testament provide lengthy accounts of Jesus' crucifixion. One scholar observed that all of them are "passion narratives with extended introductions." That certainly fits our study of Luke's Gospel as we have followed Jesus to Jerusalem. Think back through the sessions. How did you know that Jesus was on his way to his death? Explore why his death is not the end of his ministry, but rather accomplishes or fulfills it.

Bonus Activity:

Ask learners to think about other people who may have been wrongly punished or put to death because they were misunderstood or were caught in the crosshairs of a political struggle. What motives are often at the heart of such forms of injustice?

Tip:

All Christians must be reminded that Jesus was a Jew, his people were Jewish, and all the characters in the story are Jewish, except the Romans. Unfortunately, for various reasons, that also means that anti–Jewish or anti–Semitic prejudice arose in the Christian church against Jews, who ancestors were said to be "the ones who killed Jesus." While it is true that certain religious leaders opposed Jesus in his time, all of Jesus' closest followers were Jewish. Christians and Jews share a faith in one same God.

Bonus Activity:

Some interpreters find the "theology of the cross" even stronger in the Gospel of Mark because of its stark account of Jesus' death. Jesus' only articulate word from the cross in Mark's account is his loud cry, *"Eloi, Eloi, lema sabachthani?"* (Mark 15:34). Those who minister to people in desperately difficult circumstances have found that Mark's frightening account of Jesus' death offers the assurance that Jesus has also experienced the most profound human suffering, even God's apparent abandonment.

Tip:

If you have copies of Luther's Small Catechism, you might have learners use them for question #2. The "Small Catechism of Martin Luther" is also found in ELW, pp. 1160–1167.

Bonus Activity:

Gather two or three crosses from your congregation's worship center, classrooms, or publications and compare the visual, emotional and artistic impact of each of them.

Lutheran Context

1. Martin Luther taught the "theology of the cross," emphasizing both the dire reality of Jesus' gruesome death and the profound salvation that God accomplished through it. The "theology of the cross" is strong medicine for us and our human condition. The media often create public excitement about "The Gospel of Thomas" or some "newly discovered" Gnostic gospel. Almost none of those accounts, even from early centuries, pays attention to Jesus' crucifixion. Some even deny that it happened. Those other gospels may provide winsome wisdom from Jesus as a teacher, but compared to the biblical "theology of the cross," they are only mild cures for mild diseases.

• How is Jesus' death the ultimate revelation of God's profound salvation for us?

• Why is the cross so important to our understanding of Jesus' mission?

2. In his explanation to the second article of the Apostles' Creed in the Small Catechism, Luther says the following about Jesus:

> He has redeemed me, a lost and condemned human being. He has purchased and freed me from all sins, from death, and from the power of the devil, not with gold or silver but with his holy, precious blood and with his innocent suffering and death. He has done all this in order that I may belong to him, live under him in his kingdom, and serve him in eternal righteousness, innocence, and blessedness, just as he is risen from the dead and lives and rules eternally.

• What stands out to you in these words?

• Without the cross, would these words be "true"? Why or why not?

Devotional Context

1. You need to read all four Gospels to see how each evangelist highlights one or more of Jesus' "seven last words" from the cross. Luke reports three of these words at very critical points in our story (Luke 23:34, 43, 46). Note that the first "word" (verse 34) is generally printed in brackets in our Bibles because several ancient Greek copies or manuscripts did not include it, and the narrative flows smoothly without quoting Jesus. What Jesus is quoted as saying, however, fits deeply with Luke's testimony, and some scholars propose that this "word" was dropped by Gentile anti-Jewish scribes who doubted God's forgiveness for Jesus' executioners, or even for all Jews.

Listen to hear each of these words, as if you are standing at the foot of the cross.

- The first is the word of forgiveness (verse 34), spoken during the cruel, inhuman execution. How does Jesus' bond with the Father focus his mission of love? Also listen to Jesus' prayer to God on the Mount of Olives in Luke 22:42. Where has the depth of such forgiveness touched your life, your family, or your congregation?

- The second word (verse 43) is the granting of God's promise of paradise to an unworthy criminal who trusts Jesus as both are in the throes of dying. Where have you seen such unlikely faith? How strong is Christ Jesus to speak comfort during his own suffering?

- The third word (verse 46) is rich in the faith that Jesus is enveloped in God's Spirit. In Greek, the word for "spirit" is *pneuma*—like the word for the breath of our lungs or the pneumatic air in our tires—and the same word is used in Greek for saying, "he breathed his last." So Jesus returned the breath of God and then breathed his last, or gave his "spirit" to God and then "expired." Here is the unity of Jesus with God in "spirit," in purpose, in love, embodied in Jesus' life and breath as a mortal human. What do you think of the idea that Jesus gave his "spirit" to God? How does that relate to his mission?

2. When Jesus later sends the "Holy Spirit" upon the church, it is God's powerful Breath (Acts 1:4-5, 8; 2:1-4). Describe a time when you saw "the breath of life" animate someone in peril or when a dear one returned their breath to God as they "expired."

3. Through the centuries, believers have learned that the best way to testify to what God was doing in Jesus' death is not to "explain it" as if we could read God's mind, but to join the centurion in "praising God" for a wonder too deep to understand with mortal reason.

- Read Philippians 2:5-11. This may be the earliest Christian hymn we still have in praise of the "mind that was in Christ Jesus," confident that Jesus is truly enacting God's way of ruling in heaven and on earth. What strikes you about these words? What might it have to say about being a follower of Jesus?

Tip:

Do not be afraid if people begin to fear that God is unfair. They may have been wondering about that from their own experience and now are troubled about why Jesus had to endure such suffering. God's love is again more than fair because we need more than justice from God to be saved.

Bonus Activity:

Provide paper and colored markers. You might also provide old magazine, scissors, and glue for those who wish to use "pictures" rather than drawing. Invite learners to illustrate one of the three "words" of Jesus from the cross in a way that provides a unique perspective on the meaning of Jesus' words or actions.

Tip:
The next session will recount Jesus' resurrection. The wonder will continue.

Tip:
Singing or reciting a hymn reminds us that the gospel is not just an idea. God's love brings a transformation of the heart and the will. Another way to conclude this session would be to sing a classic Christian hymn such as "Jesus Shall Reign" (ELW 434) or "If You But Trust in God to Guide You" (ELW 769).

Wrap-up

1. If there are any questions to explore further, write them on chart paper or a whiteboard. Ask for volunteers to do further research to share with the group at the next session.

2. Help people take joy in the mystery of God's love revealed in Jesus' brutal death. This is not a story where a heroic figure escapes at the last minute. We are finally awed at a mercy beyond our understanding. A hymn such as "What Wondrous Love Is This?" (ELW 666) captures this theme well.

Pray

To sustain Luke's witness to the anguish and hope of Jesus' death, pray or sing the great hymn for Holy Week, "Ah, Holy Jesus" (ELW 349):

Ah, holy Jesus, how hast thou offended that we to judge thee have in hate pretended? By foes derided, by thine own rejected, O most afflicted.

Who was the guilty? Who brought this upon thee? Alas, my treason, Jesus, hath undone thee. 'Twas I, Lord Jesus, I it was denied thee; I crucified thee.

Lo, the Good Shepherd for the sheep is offered; the slave hath sinned, and the Son hath suffered; for our atonement, while we nothing heeded, God interceded.

For me, kind Jesus, was thine incarnation, thy mortal sorrow, and thy life's oblation; thy death of anguish and thy bitter passion, for my salvation.

Therefore, kind Jesus, since I cannot pay thee, I do adore thee, and will every pray thee; think on thy pity and thy love unswerving, not my deserving.
Amen.

Extending the Conversation (5 minutes)

Homework

1. Read the next session's Bible text: Luke 24:13–35.

2. Place a cross on your nightstand during the coming week, then recite each of Jesus' last words as Luke reported them, listening for God's promises to you:
"Father, forgive them; for they do not know what they are doing!"
"Truly I tell you, today you will be with me in Paradise."
"Father, into your hands I commend my spirit."

3. Do some research on the lives of Herod Antipas and Pontius Pilate. Report your findings to the class next week.

Enrichment

1. If you wish to read through the entire book of Luke during this unit, read the following sections this week:

   Day 1: Luke 21:1–19

   Day 2: Luke 21:20–36

   Day 3: Luke 21:37–22:13

   Day 4: Luke 22:14–34

   Day 5: Luke 22:35–53

   Day 6: Luke 22:54–71

   Day 7: Luke 23:1–25

2. In session 5, we explored Jesus' transfiguration on the mountain and discussed the "exodus" or "departure" that Jesus "was about to accomplish at Jerusalem" (Luke 9:31). During your reading this week of Luke 22:1–34 (days 3 and 4 on the schedule above), remember the Passover as the story of Israel's exodus from slavery.

• How did Jesus accomplish a new liberation for all people?

• How is Judas' betrayal of Jesus (Luke 22:3–6, 47–48) different from Peter's denial (Luke 22:54–62)? Have you ever been betrayed? Have you ever denied your faith in Jesus? How does Jesus' love for Peter give you hope?

3. All Christians must be reminded that Jesus was a Jew, his people were Jewish, and all the characters in the story (except the Romans) are Jewish. Like many prophetic voices in Israel's history, Jesus and the evangelist call Israel to repentance (see also Peter in Acts 2:22–36). But all of God's people, including Peter and the disciples, were complicit in Jesus' death, and as Peter proclaimed in Acts 2:39, "the promise is for you, for your children, and for all who are far away, everyone whom the Lord our God calls to him." Someone may wish to investigate the rich discussion among scholars about how this Jewish story eventually was misinterpreted as anti-Jewish or anti-Semitic.

For Further Reading

The Gospel According to Luke by Michael F. Patella in New Collegeville Bible Commentary Series (Collegeville, MN: Liturgical Press, 2005), pp. 147–152.

"Session 11: The King of the Jews" in *Learning Luke: The Apostolic Gospel* with David L. Tiede and friends (www.selectlearning.org).

Provoking the Gospel of Luke: A Storyteller's Commentary by Richard W. Swanson (Cleveland: Pilgrim Press, 2006), pp. 128–139.

Augsburg Commentary on the New Testament: Luke by David L. Tiede (Minneapolis: Augsburg Fortress, 1988), pp. 411–427.

Looking Ahead

1. Read the next session's Bible text: Luke 24:13–35.

2. Read through the Leader Guide for the next session and mark portions you wish to highlight for the group.

3. Make a checklist of any materials you'll need to do the Bonus Activities.

4. Pray for members of your group during the week.

Luke 24:13–35

Leader Session Guide

Focus Statement

The world is changed in the light of Jesus' resurrection. Israel's Scriptures testify from the past. The new age of the resurrection of the righteous has dawned in the present. The future is now the arena for the repentance and forgiveness of all the nations.

Key Verse

They said to each other, "Were not our hearts burning within us while he was talking to us on the road, while he was opening the scriptures to us?"
Luke 24:32

Focus Image

© SoFood / SuperStock

How Did Jesus' Resurrection Change the World?

Session Preparation

Before You Begin . . .

This story in Luke's Gospel marks the fulfillment and transformation of everything that Jesus has been doing as God's Messiah. Take time to appreciate the deeply human experience of the disciples and how Jesus' resurrection sustains God's profound regard for the body. In the resurrection, God confirms or vindicates Jesus as Messiah, and Jesus prepares his followers for the mission which lies ahead.

Session Instructions

1. Read this Session Guide completely and highlight or underline any portions you wish to emphasize with the group. Note any Bonus Activities you wish to do.

2. If you plan to do any special activities, check to see what materials you'll need, if any.

3. Have extra Bibles on hand in case a member of the group forgets to bring one.

4. Take some time to consider what the group may wish to study next. Explore all the Book of Faith options available.

Session Overview

Jesus' resurrection is not only a fact in the past. It is a **transformative** event for the present and future. "I want to know Christ," says Paul, "and the power of his resurrection" (Philippians 3:10). Luke's story leads us deeply into how the experience of Jesus' resurrected presence turned fearful followers into apostolic witnesses.

LITERARY CONTEXT

This story deserves to be savored, not hurried, so that its power can be experienced. Moving directly inside the narrative may also divert or at least defer the anxious modern question, "How can you prove this?" Don't be afraid of that question, although you won't ultimately be able to "prove" Jesus' resurrection in some scientific way. The story makes it clear that the disciples were fearful and awed in the face of something that had never happened before, or since, until God's great day still coming. Let the story do its own

? *Transformative:*

This word is chosen to communicate the Christian conviction that Jesus' resurrection truly changes everything. An electrical transformer can change direct current to alternating current. Some Christian theologians follow Paul in speaking of the Christian life as "a new creation," as if God remade the world. The point is that Jesus' resurrection is different from Lazarus being revived. God is doing a new thing, which will only be finished in the resurrection at the last day.

work, drawing people into a wondrous event where "believing is seeing," instead of the usual other way around.

The suggestions in the Learner Session Guide are intended to create space for people to speak about their own experiences of God's presence in encounters with strangers, hearing God's voice in the reading of scripture, and knowing Christ's presence in the sacrament. They know the power of these experiences, even though most people don't talk about them for fear of sounding peculiar. But Luke's story and the suggested activities are invitations to people who think they can explain everything rationally to "suspend disbelief." In the next story, Luke also says of the disciples that "in their joy they were disbelieving and still wondering" (24:41).

In the story of the rich ruler, Jesus notes that it is not impossible even for a rich person to be saved because "What is impossible for mortals is possible for God" (Luke 18:27). Try to set a tone in which people can experience the story and relate to it personally without skeptical arguments about what is or is not possible. Everybody knows from all their experiences that dead people stay dead, and Jesus' disciples knew that too. Yet the crucified Jesus appeared among them alive, embodied in a transformed body, and teaching them how to read the scriptures fulfilled in him. The world was changed.

HISTORICAL CONTEXT

This story is historically alive, inviting exploration of Jesus' crucifixion and resurrection, when Luke was writing this narrative of "the things that have been fulfilled among us," and now, when the power of Christ's resurrection remains the world's hope.

Luke's account gives us a clear glimpse into the dangerous context facing the travelers to Emmaus. The Roman execution of Jesus by crucifixion was explicitly intended to quash any hopes that "he was the one to redeem Israel" (24:21). As will also be evident in the stories in Acts, Jesus' followers faced imprisonment, flogging, and even death if they went around "proclaiming that in Jesus there is the resurrection of the dead" (Acts 4:2, 10; 5:17; 6–8:1). Evidently, Jesus' resurrection was not good news to the authorities.

By the time the evangelist wrote this book, Jerusalem had probably been destroyed by the Romans, and the followers of Jesus were being excluded regularly from many synagogues. Acts identifies Paul as an apostle (Acts 14:4,14), but he was falsely accused by the authorities in Jerusalem of teaching the Jews among the Gentiles to forsake Moses (Acts 21:21). Luke reports that "beginning with Moses and all the prophets," the risen Jesus "interpreted to them the things about himself in all the scriptures" (Luke 24:27). The Jews who were not followers of Jesus were strict in their interpretation of "**Moses and the prophets**," and Jesus' apostles insisted that Jesus truly fulfilled all of God's promises (2 Corinthians 1:20). Luke's account of what the risen Jesus taught was a powerful testimony in the late first century.

Our historical context (see Devotional Context) also resists and resents the testimony of Jesus' lordship because Jesus' resurrection calls us to turn from our idols of power and privilege, that is, to repent and believe that God has vindicated Jesus as God's way. Christians are right to love the promise of their resurrection in Jesus. Luke's witness to our context, however, also calls us to witness and service according to Jesus' way of mercy and justice, personally and together. Jesus' resurrection is good news as a promise to fearful and sinful people (see Acts 2:38–39) as the Holy Spirit transforms us from being self-centered into becoming Jesus' apostles.

Lutheran Context

Lutherans emphasize the "**theology of the cross**" to the extent that they are often thought to be more "Good Friday Christians" than "Easter Christians." It might be true that the glorious Easter celebrations of the Greek Orthodox churches outshine those of the Lutherans. The intense joy and deep perplexity of Luke's story, however, reminds all Christians that Good Friday is only "good" because of Easter, and Easter joy is still grounded in human realities of "looking sad" and "disbelieving and still wondering" in joy (Luke 24:17,41). The Easter gospel is not about bunnies and springtime; it is the story of God's vindication of the crucified Messiah. Easter is not the denial of death but its conquest.

In faithfulness to their identity, therefore, Lutheran congregations are places where the celebration of the resurrection of Jesus is filled with the joy that does not forget Jesus' mission and death. Those who have suffered losses and

 Moses and the Prophets:

In the first century, Israel's Scriptures were written on scrolls that were stored in boxes in the synagogues, not bound in books. The word *Bible* means "book," but the synagogues had scrolls of the five books of Moses (also called the Torah or law), plus scrolls of the prophets and some other writings. Jesus is interpreting his own work as Messiah as the fulfillment of Israel's Scriptures.

Theology of the Cross:

As discussed in Session 7, this term highlights how all four Gospels focus on Jesus' death by crucifixion as the most profound revelation of God's love, even though his execution appears to be a triumph of violence. "We proclaim Christ crucified," declared Paul (1 Corinthians 1:23).

deaths in their families will hear a genuine hope, filled with human pathos and confident of God's long-standing scriptural promises. Congregations where the Lord's Supper is celebrated on Easter are alive to the memory that this Supper was instituted "on the night he was betrayed." They confess faith in the embodied promise of the risen Christ in the bread that is broken and the wine that is poured.

Consider asking the pastor to explain how Lutheran Christians understand Christ's living presence in the Lord's Supper, taking particular time with Luke's powerful testimony that Jesus was made known to them in the breaking of the bread.

? **Repent:**

This rich biblical word means more than "feel sorry" or become penitent. It is the word for "turning" and "returning" to God. Thus, it is a gift of God's mercy to "give repentance" in that those who are unworthy are lovingly called back into God's love.

Lutheran emphasis on "the forgiveness of sins" is also faithful to Luke's story in which Jesus' resurrection is announced by the apostle Peter to be God's renewed invitation to all people to return in faith (**repent**) and receive God's forgiveness in trust (faith). God's promise doesn't stop with the insiders, but raising Jesus is central to God's way of extending this renewal to all people (Acts 2:37–42). Therefore, whether in a first-century synagogue or a twenty-first-century congregation, no group can possess this faith as their own, because Jesus' resurrection is God's intervention to bless "everyone whom the Lord our God calls to him" (Acts 2:39).

The Lutheran Reformation rests on two pillars: the forgiveness of sinners; and the calling of every Christian to be the hands and feet of Christ, serving the neighbor and the world. To grasp these two convictions, call attention to how early in every Sunday worship the congregation is invited to confess their sins to receive forgiveness and how the worship service concludes with sending the faithful to "Go in peace and serve the Lord." To hear how God is already at work in the daily lives of the faithful, take time in small groups to ask one another, "How is that part about 'serving the Lord' going for you?"

DEVOTIONAL CONTEXT

The biblical witness to Jesus' resurrection is filled with awe, thanksgiving to God, and hope in the resurrection of all who belong to Christ Jesus. It is not a scientific account of "what really happened" but a witness to what God was truly doing. The Bible is realistic about death and dying of mortal human beings yet full of faith that this life is "not all there is." Paul even said, "If for this life only we have hoped in Christ, we are of all people most to be pitied" (1 Corinthians 15:19).

It may seem strange to commend attention to worship services of Christian burial in the session about the resurrection, but this story is about God raising the dead, not about human immortality. Furthermore, we are not given extensive or extravagant visions of heaven or paradise, but at this point in the Gospel, the risen Christ is still down to earth.

Thus, the suggestion of exploring the vocations of health professionals also fits. In the ancient church, the Christians were famous for staying in plague-ridden cities because their neighbors were suffering. The Christians were not afraid of death, even their own death. The resurrection of Jesus inspires courage in the face of death.

Facilitator's Prayer

Lord Jesus, the hearts of your disciples burned within them as you spoke with them and opened the scriptures to them. Light that fire in my heart and in the hearts of your disciples who are gathered in our Book of Faith study of Luke. Give us new eyes to see, hands to touch, and minds to understand your presence among us. Amen.

Gather (10–15 minutes)

Check-in

Invite learners to share completed homework or any new thoughts or insights about the previous session. Be ready to give a brief recap of that session if necessary.

Pray

O God, whose blessed Son made himself known to his disciples in the breaking of bread, open the eyes of our faith, that we may behold him in all his redeeming work, Jesus Christ, our Savior and Lord, who lives and reigns with you and the Holy Spirit, one God, now and forever. Amen.
(Prayer for the evening of Easter Day, ELW, p. 32)

Focus Activity

Share with at least one other person what you recall to be one of the most memorable meals you ever had. What made it memorable? Was it the food, the person or people you were with, the purpose for the meal, or something that happened during the meal?

 Tip:
A Bible standing open would be a good focal point, along with an uncut loaf of bread.

 Tip:
As an alternative to the Focus Activity, you might consider doing the following: Place a whole, uncut loaf of bread and a closed Bible on the table in front of the group. Pick up the loaf of bread, hold it high, unbroken, for all to see, then break the loaf with the words, "Reveal yourself to us, O Lord, as once you revealed yourself to your disciples in the breaking of the bread." Then lift high the Bible, open it, and say, "Open the scriptures to us, living Lord, as you did with the disciples on the road to Emmaus."

This alternative Focus Activity may seem rather dramatic, but relax and do it in your own way. It is most important that people sense your awe or reverence in the opening of the scriptures and the breaking of the bread.

Tip:

You could also do the reading dramatically using the volunteers to read the following parts: Narrator, Jesus, Cleopas, Second Voice.

Tip:

In John's account, the disciples know it is Jesus but are afraid to ask him if it is true. This is the third time Jesus appeared to the disciples after the resurrection in John's Gospel.

Tip:

This is probably not the time to be clever about "seeing and not seeing." The prophetic diagnosis is that our blindness is due to hardness of heart, not merely the psychology of perception.

Bonus Activity:

Ask learners to look at the Focus Image on p. 57 in their session guides. Bread is a common food in almost all cultures, and "breaking bread" together is routine. Somehow, by God's presence in the ordinary, Jesus was "made known to them in the breaking of the bread" (verse 35). The evangelist doesn't tell us how this happened. But God revealed or made Jesus known to the same people whose eyes had been "kept from recognizing him" (verse 16). Ask: How have you experienced God's presence in common, everyday ways?

Open Scripture (10–15 minutes)

One reader, perhaps a man because of the reference to the women in verse 24, could read verses 13–27. The second reader, perhaps a woman to balance the testimony as Luke also does, could read verses 28–35.

Read Luke 24:13–35.

- What images or words stood out for you in this story?
- What was surprising or confusing?
- Why do you think Luke tells this particular story?

Join the Conversation (25–55 minutes)

Literary Context

1. This story is another literary masterpiece from the writer of Luke. None of the other Gospels mentions these events, but the risen Jesus also gave bread and fish to his disciples by the shore in John's Gospel (John 21:9–13). Compare this story in Luke to John's story. What similarities do you see?

2. Luke's story draws us deeply into the mystery of why people are often so blind to what is truly happening. This human reality is also commonly depicted in tragic dramas when someone fails to see what is obvious to the audience.

- The two followers don't recognize Jesus at first. How does that fact add to the impact of the end of the story?

3. The prophets of Israel often spoke of the "spiritual blindness" of God's people. They saw that blindness as a sign of human self-absorption. In this story in Luke, the risen Messiah teaches his disciples how God is at work in what is happening, whether people see it or not. The word *disciples* literally means "learners." Notice that Jesus teaches his followers/learners from "Moses and all the prophets" even before they recognize who he is. We know that "Jesus himself" is walking with them (verse 15), but they don't recognize him; in fact, they can't because "their eyes were kept from recognizing him" (verse 16). They only recognize him for who he is when "their eyes were opened" (verse 31) and as he "took bread, blessed and broke it, and gave it to them" (verse 30).

- How do you feel when it says, "Their eyes were kept from recognizing him"? What or who do you imagine prevented their recognition of Jesus?

• What or who "opened their eyes"?

4. When the Scriptures are read regularly in public worship, they often seem routine, but sometimes we are touched in ways we had not expected. Recalling what they felt before they knew it was Jesus, these disciples "said to each other, 'Were not our hearts burning within us while he was talking to us on the road, while he was opening the scriptures to us?'" When John Wesley heard a reading of Luther's commentary on Galatians, his heart was "strangely warmed" in awareness of God's unexpected presence. Has that ever happened to you or to someone you know?

Historical Context

1. Take a look at the map "Palestine in Jesus' Time" on p. 8. Notice how close Emmaus was to Jerusalem. What do you suppose the people in Jerusalem and the surrounding area were saying about the events related to Jesus' death? What does Cleopas' question (24:18) seem to imply?

2. Jesus' resurrection is both an historical event (because it happened at a specific time in human history) and a disruption when God's future broke into human history. When the widow's son at Nain was revived from death, the people declared, "A great prophet has risen among us!" and "God has looked favorably on his people" (Luke 7:16). The young man probably went back to his life when "Jesus gave him to his mother" (7:15). But Jesus' resurrection was an event that changed the world, marking the fulfillment of all of Israel's history and the dawn of God's apostolic mission of the church.

• How is this story from Luke a glimpse into a world where everything has changed? Notice the wonder and confusion of the people who were still disappointed, afraid, and awed.

• If local newspapers had existed, do you think Jesus' death would have been front-page news? Why or why not?

3. A second historical context for this story is the time when Luke wrote his "orderly account of the events that have been fulfilled among us" (Luke 1:1) sometime in the late first century, probably about fifty years or so after Jesus' resurrection. About forty years after Jesus' resurrection, the Romans destroyed the temple in Jerusalem during a Jewish uprising.

• How do you suppose this story sounded to Jesus' followers after the Romans had destroyed the temple, Israel was scattered, and the Jesus movement was expanding?

Tip:
This is another place to be careful about not blaming "the Jews." We are listening in on a struggle among groups for how Israel can be faithful. Although the stories in Acts reflect a deep division among the people of Israel, all the players are still Jewish at this point in the story, including all of the followers of Jesus.

Bonus Activity:
Role-play the conversation on the road to Emmaus with particular attention to the direct quotes of the travelers.

Tip:

The New Testament is full of Israel's Scriptures, and all of Israel shared the first five books of "Moses" and the prophets, although not all groups had the same "writings." By studying Jesus' scriptural responses to the devil (Luke 4:1–13) and his address in Nazareth (Luke 4:16–30), you could begin to see Luke's powerful depiction of Jesus as an interpreter of scripture. Jesus' followers agreed with their Jewish relatives and friends on the sacredness of the scriptures, but they interpreted those scriptures in the light of Jesus' fulfillment of them.

Bonus Activity:

Since this is the final session centered in Luke, this could be a time for the pastor to celebrate the Lord's Supper with the group, using Luke 24:28–35 as the Gospel text.

Tip:

Lutheran interpretation of the Scriptures is focused on what they tell us about God and—more profoundly—how the living God addresses us in our hearing of the Scriptures. This story is filled with the mystery of divine presence, in the resurrected Jesus, in the clear conviction that God raised Jesus for a purpose, and in the anticipation of the coming of the Holy Spirit. With those things in mind, you might explore these questions together: 1) How does this story speak to me? 2) Do I hear God's word for me, for us, for the world? 3) Am I challenged or convicted? 4) Am I assured or empowered?

4. Notice how thoroughly the story is filled with Israel's Scriptures, what Christians refer to as the "Old Testament." It's important to remember that Jesus' scriptures were scriptures of Israel.

• Imagine you are a Christian preacher in Rome. If you picked up and expanded upon Jesus' own words, "Then beginning with Moses and all the prophets, he interpreted to them the things about himself in all the scriptures" (24:27), what would you say?

Lutheran Context

1. Using the principle of scripture interpreting scripture, explore how the resurrection is described in the following passages. How do these passages shed light on the meaning of the resurrected Jesus?

• John 11:17–27

• 1 Corinthians 15:12–23

2. Jesus' followers recognized Jesus when he broke bread and gave it to them (Luke 24:30). Think about how the Lord's Supper, Holy Communion, is celebrated in worship in your church.

• How would you compare the sharing of bread, Christ's body, in the sacrament to what happened in the meal Jesus shared with the two followers?

• Think about the people who visit your congregation at Easter. Maybe they come for family events or because they hope to hear a word of hope. The music and flowers are lovely. You are now among Jesus' disciples who know that he is alive. How can you and your congregation be his "apostles" to the visitors, recognizing the presence of the living Lord in the opening of the scriptures and the breaking of bread?

3. The Lutheran tradition specializes in thanksgiving for the forgiveness of sins and in trusting God's calling of all Christians in their homes and families, their public lives, their paid and unpaid work, and their communities of worship. At the close of worship, the pastor routinely says, "Go in peace. Serve the Lord!" and the people respond, "Thanks be to God!"

• Since Jesus is risen from the dead, it is time to ask each other, "How is that part about serving the Lord going for you?"

Devotional Context

1. We talked about two different historical "contexts" for understanding the story. A third historical context is the "here and now." Jesus not only came back from the dead, but he has also been vindicated as God's true Messiah and Lord of heaven and earth for all time and eternity. Jesus also continues to make himself known to us in his Word and in the breaking of bread of the Lord's Supper.

- As you go into your life in the world, including your places of work and play, what difference does it make that Jesus died and God raised him from the dead?

- What helps you to recognize God at work in your life and to see Jesus for who he is?

2. Look again at the Focus Image for this session. What do you see? Who is the person holding the bread? What's his "story"? How has Jesus been made known to you in the breaking of bread?

3. Describe a time when you had a rich, spiritual conversation with a stranger. Maybe you even discussed your hopes and disappointments as you felt drawn to say things or ready to hear things you had not discussed with anyone. Maybe it was on a plane or at a camp or cruise where you were traveling together without previously knowing each other. As you listen in on the conversation of these travelers on the road to Emmaus, do you recall times when you experienced God's unexpected presence among strangers?

4. Jesus' resurrection shines God's light of promise into all of life because death is no longer ultimate. If you read the prayers in the Service of Christian Burial, you will notice how realistic Christian funerals are about the decay of the mortal body. But they also rejoice in the confidence in the sure and certain hope of the resurrection.

- What person do you know, or have you known, who is the best example of one who lives in the sure and certain hope of the resurrection?

Tip:
Keep your eyes on Jesus as you explore this holy story. The disciples are just catching up and so are Jesus' followers in the present time. This story does not instruct us in how we are supposed to behave. It reveals how God is at work, down to earth.

Tip:
Remember to entrust all the participants to God. You can't control their responses anyway, and God is good for it.

Tip:
Jesus' resurrection is our sure and certain hope in death, but also in life. As an evangelist once said, "Jesus does not make us so heavenly minded that we are of no earthly good."

Wrap–up

1. If there are any questions to explore further, write them on chart paper or a whiteboard. Ask for volunteers to do further research to share with the group at the next session.

2. We say that Jesus' resurrection changes the world.
- How does Jesus invite you to draw close to the living God?
- How does Jesus empower you for sharing God's love with others?
- Who do you know who also needs Jesus' acceptance and strength?

Pray

Lord Jesus, we journey with your disciples in awe and wonder at your resurrection. You have been vindicated as Messiah, Lord, and Savior, for us and for the world. Open the eyes of our hearts, Lord, to recognize you among us in your word, in the opening of the Scriptures, and in the breaking of bread. We thank you for our bodies, and we praise you that we are already enfolded in the life of your resurrected body until the time we are raised from the dead ourselves. In you, we catch a glimpse of the world to come, but we rejoice here and now to be sent as your people into this world you so love. In your holy name, we pray. Amen.

Extending the Conversation (5 minutes)

Homework

1. Consider going back over parts of Luke's Gospel that were not covered in this study. Use what you have learned in this course to "inform" your own study and reading of Luke.

2. What part of the Bible would you like to know more about? Give some thought to what you might like to read or study next.

Enrichment

1. Luke's story of Jesus reaches a crescendo in his resurrection, but it does not stop there because God is not done with the world. Read the rest of Luke 24 and continue on in the Acts of the Apostles to see how Jesus' resurrection paves the way for the Holy Spirit to empower the church in God's continuing mission of promise and hope for all.

Notice in Peter's sermon on Pentecost that the pouring out of the Spirit is a sign of the fulfillment of God's scriptural promise of an inspired people and the opening of the doors of salvation to "everyone who calls on the name of the Lord" (Acts 2:14–21). Notice also how Peter's announcement of the resurrection of the crucified Messiah first strikes fear in the people, "What shall we do?" But Jesus' resurrection is an invitation to return to God (repent) with baptism, "for the promise is for you, for your children, and for all who are far away, everyone whom the Lord our God calls to him." (Acts 2:36–39).

If you wish to complete your reading of the entire book of Luke and see how it flows into its sequel, The Acts of the Apostles, read the following sections this week.

Day 1: Luke 24:1–12

Day 2: Luke 24:36–41

Day 3: Luke 24:44–53

Day 4: Acts 1:1–11

Day 5: Acts 1:12–26

Day 6: Acts 2:1–21

Day 7: Acts 2:22–47

2. Interview a nurse or physician about how his or her care of people expresses God's love for human bodies, including the tender care for those who are dying in hospice. Christian ministries of healing have always trusted God's love for the body without pretending that mortal humans will live forever. Offer prayers of thanksgiving for those who care for the sick, the elderly, and the dying.

• How did Jesus accomplish a new liberation for all people?

For Further Reading

The Gospel According to Luke by Michael F. Patella in New Collegeville Bible Commentary Series (Collegeville, MN: Liturgical Press, 2005), pp. 153–158.

"Session 12: Crucified and Raised" in *Learning Luke: The Apostolic Gospel* with David L. Tiede and friends (www.selectlearning.org).

Provoking the Gospel of Luke: A Storyteller's Commentary by Richard W. Swanson (Cleveland: Pilgrim Press, 2006), pp. 139–146.

Augsburg Commentary on the New Testament: Luke by David L. Tiede (Minneapolis: Augsburg Fortress, 1988), pp. 432–444.

Looking Ahead

1. Alert participants to the delight of reading Acts after Luke.

2. Identify any next steps that are planned to follow this study.

3. Encourage participants to pray for each other and for the empowerment of God's people to be a blessing in the world.